Heaven Scent

Dr. J. Franklin Tillery

authorHOUSE®

AuthorHouse™
1663 Liberty Drive
Bloomington, IN 47403
www.authorhouse.com
Phone: 833-262-8899

This book is a work of non-fiction. Unless otherwise noted, the author and the publisher
make no explicit guarantees as to the accuracy of the information contained in this book
and in some cases, names of people and places have been altered to protect their privacy.

Published by AuthorHouse 08/27/2024

ISBN: 979-8-8230-1764-0 (sc)
ISBN: 979-8-8230-1765-7 (hc)
ISBN: 979-8-8230-1763-3 (e)

Library of Congress Control Number: 2023923940

Print information available on the last page.

Interior Image Credit: John Tillery

Scripture taken from the King James Version of the Bible.

Scripture quotations are from The Holy Bible, English Standard Version®
(ESV®), copyright © 2001 by Crossway, a publishing ministry of Good
News Publishers. Used by permission. All rights reserved.

Scripture taken from the Holy Bible, NEW INTERNATIONAL VERSION®. Copyright ©
1973, 1978, 1984, 2011 by Biblica, Inc. All rights reserved worldwide. Used by permission. NEW
INTERNATIONAL VERSION® and NIV® are registered trademarks of Biblica, Inc. Use of either
trademark for the offering of goods or services requires the prior written consent of Biblica US, Inc.

This book is printed on acid-free paper.

Contents

DEDICATION

To my wife,
Barbara.
My loyal journey toward recovery partner!

To my daughters,
Michelle, Marie, Melinda, and Shawntell.
True blessings from my Father!

To my grandchildren,
Micah, Tabitha, Samuel, Elijah,
Lance, Caleb, Gabriel, Alexander,
Nathan, Steven, Jessie, and Jewel.
Side by side, or miles apart, you will always be close to my heart!

Also, to my "adopted" daughters.
It is a joy to be a part of your lives!

And to their children's children to the tenth generation!

When people ask, you can say,

"The cycle stopped here!"

Author's Note

ON THE FOLLOWING PAGES, WOVEN TOGETHER as clearly as I can remember them, I invite you to join me on a journey through my memories. I have made every effort to convey the following events, conversations, and emotions as accurately as possible, but as a professional counselor, I recognize the inherent subjectivity of memory.

Memories are delicate threads of personal experiences influenced by time, perspective, and the nuances of perception. What I recount here is a version of events filtered through the lens of my recollections. Others who were present during the exact moments, like my two brothers, may remember them differently. They were there with me, but in a significant emotional way, they were not present.

My aim is to offer a glimpse into the tapestry of my life as I remember it. Nothing is dressed up; to be perfectly frank, publishing guidelines are such that I've needed to tone down my writing. If you know me, you understand that I'm not given to embellishment, so please approach these recollections with an open mind.

Thank you for joining me on my journey toward recovery. I hope my memories spark reflections on the nature of recollection itself. For by sharing the stories, and the myriad ways our lives intersect with those of others, our burdens are lightened.

John

Acknowledgements

THE ARMY, CHRIST, AND THE LOVE OF A GOOD WOMAN

I JOINED THE UNITED STATES Army on January 11, 1972. While enlisted, the Army instilled in me important values like discipline, integrity, loyalty, duty, honor, teamwork, accountability, communication skills, and a love for my country. The Army gave me the structure to set aside self-destructive behavior and adopt positive coping mechanisms: I stopped drinking, smoking, and engaging in high-risk behaviors. **Without the Army, my life would have turned out very differently.**

While in the Army and stationed in Alaska, I found faith in God and accepted Christ as my Savior. This decision gave me eternal life, forgiveness, purpose, community, freedom, hope, and the Holy Spirit. The storms in my mind calmed, the doubts subsided, and hope was born. **Without Christ, my life would have taken a dark path.**

In 1976, I married a wonderful woman who shared my beliefs, made me a better person, and brought joy, laughter, and love to my life. Barbara is the embodiment of trust and adds sparkle to my world. **Without her, my story would not be complete.**

Foreword

John's Brother

WE WERE MORE COMPETITORS THAN COLLABORATORS. The best way to explain our childhood can be found in William Golding's novel, *The Lord of the Flies*. Set amidst the turmoil of war, a plane evacuating British schoolboys was downed over a deserted tropical island.

Initially they relished their freedom without adults, but soon the boys grappled with the challenges of survival, so they elected Ralph as their leader and Jack as the one in charge of hunting. Ralph built a signal fire to attract any passing ships, yet he faced resistance as the hunters, led by Jack, prioritized the thrill of hunting.

When the boys discovered that the signal fire had somehow been extinguished, fear and accusations quickly spread among the boys. A hunting expedition ensued, tensions rose, the group fractured, and three of the boys were killed.

One night, as the boys slept, a military paratrooper landed on the island and found the boys. Overwhelmed by the realization of their descent into savagery, all the boys weep as the officer, oblivious to the true horrors, offered them comfort.

Much of what happened on that island was true in our childhood. Well, all but the rescue. However, through all the traumas, I believe something, perhaps a hardened resilience, was built into us.

Steve

Introduction

A well-chosen anthology is a complete dispensary of
medicine for the more common mental disorders
and may be used as much for prevention as cure.
—Robert Graves[1]

THIS BOOK IS A COLLECTION OF EVENTS AND
memories written in a style that would be easy for my children and
grandchildren to read. In fact, I wrote this book with them in mind. It is
more of an anthology than an autobiography. An anthology is a collection
of writings, often written by multiple authors, that are grouped together
because they share a common theme or subject matter. Although, in this
case, my anthology has only one author, and that is me. In compiling this
collection of my life experiences, I hope that my stories will inspire and
encourage. Perhaps they will offer generations to come a glimpse into a
world that is no longer visible but is still very much alive in my memories.

I postponed writing this book for many years because my childhood
memories were either too dark and depressing to revisit or simply just
unavailable to my mind. However, not unlike the nursery rhyme "Humpty
Dumpty," I have found that by collecting the broken and disconnected
shards of my memories, it is possible to gain some healing from my past.
I desire that this book will give hope to anyone struggling to find some
healing from their past trauma.

War has punctuated my life; not only in times of armed military
conflict but also the unimaginable battle that may occur inside the home
"behind friendly lines." Though the war I faced as a child was not like
a conventional war, the damages to the flesh, bone, and spirit were. I
simultaneously depended upon and feared the adults in my life, which
allowed fear to be cast deep inside me. Some of my memories are most
likely lost forever.

The experience of what happened in a World War II Nazi prisoner of war (POW) camp is more closely aligned with the war I lived through. I take comfort in their stories; if they could survive and thrive after their experiences, I could also. Though my experiences pale compared to the terror, chaos, and horrors those men, women, and children experienced, if placed on a spectrum between Main Street USA and the concentration camp in Buchenwald, Germany, I have much more in common with the latter.

In the early 2000s, I interned at the San Antonio Uniformed Services Health Education Consortium's Clinical Pastoral Education (CPE) program. While there, I learned how important it is to "journey with one another." Part of a therapist's work is to help their client in the total sense of the word. To come alongside them, to journey with them: To provide them with the hope that a past event or events need not control their present day or disturb their night.

While in the CPE program, I discovered that for years I had viewed my present and future through the lens of my past. Thus began my conscious journey toward recovery. I saw how this had interfered with almost everything in my life and why, because much of my energy was used to keep my past buried and battened down, I often felt exhausted. I have learned how to allow God and others to journey with me and can now view my past and future more clearly through the lens of the present.

Since beginning this journey toward recovery, many of my past traumas have lost their dreadful hold on me. A grip that I wasn't even aware of. For example, why was I always vigilant and angry after watching a movie at the theater? Why could I never relax on vacation? Why did I hate going into big stores? Why couldn't I sleep unless I covered my feet with a sheet? The unbelievable thing is that as memories bubbled up on my journey, I was freed from a prison I did not know I was in until the invisible bars disappeared.

The title of this book, Heaven Scent, has to do with discovering refuge, awareness, and healing. A refuge is a place or state of safety and rest where you don't have to look over your shoulder. You can sleep peacefully and make noise without worrying about being found or harmed.

During one particularly traumatic event, I found a most unlikely place of refuge: a dirty clothes hamper located in the space under the stairs in the old "garage house" we lived in for a while. Even though it always smelled of urine, by burying myself underneath piles of dirty clothes and sheets, that dirty-clothes hamper turned out to be a place of complete safety.

In 2 Corinthians 2:16 (ESV), the apostle Paul tells of both a reality and a metaphor of extraordinary convergence. "To one a fragrance from death to death, to the other a fragrance from life to life." The historical background for this verse was that when the Romans conquered in battle, they would return to the city of Rome in a long procession.[2] As they displayed the captives and wealth they had acquired, priests would lead the way, swinging incense as a thanksgiving offering to their gods. For those prisoners condemned to slavery or death, that incense was the scent of death; to those who were the victors, it was the scent of life.

On my journey toward recovery, I have found a new hiding place with a new scent, the scent of life and not death. The hiding place? In the heart and mind of God. As Isaiah 49:15 (ESV) tells us, "Can a woman forget her nursing child, that she should have no compassion on the son of her womb? Even these may forget, yet I will not forget you." Not only does God not forget, but in Psalm 56:8 (KJV), we are told that He also "stores our tears in a bottle." One day, He will tenderly and compassionately wipe away every tear from your eye and every reason to cry (Revelation 21:4 ESV). Only tears of joy will be present!

You, too, may have experienced a war of armed conflict, a war at home, or perhaps both. In this "anthology," I offer my stories of trauma and restoration to serve as a path of healing for all of you. I pray this book will help you comprehend the grace, love, and peace that God alone can and will grant. Remember always - you are not alone; there is hope.

Chapter 1

TRAUMA

This is how bad stories end.
But it's also how the best stories begin.[3]
—Iain Thomas

WHAT IS TRAUMA? THE AMERICAN PSYCHOLOGICAL Association states, "Trauma is a person's emotional response to a distressing experience. Unlike ordinary hardships, traumatic events are sudden and unpredictable, involve a serious threat to life—like bodily injury or death—and feel beyond a person's control." The article continues. "Most importantly, events are traumatic to the degree that they undermine a person's sense of safety in the world and create a sense that catastrophe could strike at any time."[4]

Most experts agree that there are five main types of trauma: acute, chronic, complex, secondary or vicarious trauma, and adverse childhood experiences (ACE).

- Acute trauma results from a single incident.
- Chronic trauma is repeated and prolonged, such as domestic violence or abuse.
- Complex trauma is exposure to varied and multiple traumatic events, often of an invasive, interpersonal nature.
- Secondary or vicarious trauma arises from exposure to other people's suffering.
- Adverse childhood experiences (ACE)[5] cover a wide range of challenging situations that children either directly face or witness before developing practical coping skills. ACEs can disrupt the

1

ordinary development course, and emotional injury can last long into adulthood.

Having experienced all of them, I have struggled to find healing and peace for most of my adult life. My journey toward recovery took flight a few years ago when a metaphor dawned on me that answered many questions about why I felt the way I did.

Movement

It happened so quickly. I was on a Zoom link with my counselor, Chris, when he asked, "What just happened? Your face changed." I was taken aback by his observation, not realizing that my emotions were so transparent. It was a difficult session, and I was struggling to keep my composure. Chris is a perceptive counselor, and I appreciate that he notices the small things. We talked about my anxiety and how it manifests itself, and he provided some helpful tools for me to manage it. It's not easy to confront your own emotions, but I'm continually grateful for Chris's guidance and support.

I glanced at my face on the computer screen and, although I couldn't tell you how, it was as if I were looking at an emotionally impacted version of myself. A sudden wave of emotions hit me, and I felt an inexplicable sensation of sadness, but at the same time, I felt that it was not quite the right word to describe what I was feeling. It was as if the emotions were too complex to be confined to a single word. Puzzled, I tried to make sense of what was happening, but I couldn't quite grasp it. After a few moments of contemplation, I finally found the words to express my feelings, "It feels like sadness, but it's not." Then, I just dismissed it as an anomaly, thinking that it was probably just a momentary glitch. Nonetheless, that experience left me feeling unsettled and wondering if there was more to it than meets the eye.

MEDUSA

One of the most poignant and powerful metaphors for childhood trauma is the Greek mythological figure of Medusa. The story of Medusa, with her writhing snakes for hair and the power to turn those who gaze upon her to stone, is a fitting representation of the enduring effects of trauma on those who experience it.

Medusa

Like Medusa's victims, those who have experienced trauma can find themselves frozen in fear, unable to move forward or escape the grip of their painful memories. The trauma can seep into every aspect of their lives, affecting their relationships, careers, and overall well-being.

Yet, just like Perseus, the hero who slayed Medusa, those who have experienced trauma can also find the strength and courage to face their fears and overcome the challenges before them. With the right support and resources, they can begin to heal and move forward, breaking free from the grip of their past and forging a new path toward a brighter future.

While all mythology seems to tend toward trauma, it also has the power to teach us how to live courageously. Just like Medusa's victims, it was as if I had been a statue of stone for the past sixty years, motionless and immobile. However, at that moment, I was experiencing something revealing but wordless, not with the mind's vocabulary but in the language of the heart. The sense of unexpected disbelief and uncertainty mingled with the sensation that I was no longer frozen in stone.

The story of Medusa captures trauma's essence and illustrates the enduring power trauma has on those who experience it. Sadly, Medusa has been reduced to a mere caricature, a mindless, vicious, horrifying monster with snakes for hair, turning people into stone, nothing else. However, Medusa is one of the most misunderstood and abused mythological characters.

In his poem Metamorphoses, Ovid put flesh and bones into her story.[6] Medusa was not always a monster. A virgin acolyte in the temple of the goddess Minerva, she was once a woman of great beauty, and her hair was the most stunning of her many charms. Countless men wanted to marry Medusa, but no man would dare try to take her by force.

It wasn't long, however, before she became an innocent victim in someone else's power struggle. Neptune, the god of freshwater and the sea, and Minerva, the virgin goddess of music, poetry, medicine, wisdom, commerce, weaving, and the crafts, constantly competed with one another.[7] This rivalry was so constant that, while flaunting his rivalrous power in front of Minerva, Neptune raped Medusa.

What was the result of being a blameless victim? Compassion? Care? No, in a jealous rage, since Minerva had no power over Neptune, she turned her venom on the one she was supposed to protect, Medusa. The victim was then retraumatized at the hands of her protector; Minerva metamorphosed Medusa into a Gorgon, a hideous monstrosity whose hair was made of snakes. Her entire existence and attraction were flattened from that day on. She was relegated to a singular label: monster. Anyone who dared look into her eyes was turned stone.

MEDUSA AS METAPHOR

"What happens to all who have experienced trauma?" This is a question that has been asked by many people who have gone through traumatic experiences. Trauma can leave deep scars on a person's psyche and can lead to a variety of negative outcomes, such as anxiety, depression, and post-traumatic stress disorder (PTSD).

One way that trauma affects people is by causing them to become emotionally numb or shut down. Like Medusa's victims who turned into stone, those who have experienced trauma may feel immobilized and disconnected from the world. They may struggle to form close relationships with others or to express their emotions, as they feel unable to trust or connect with others.

For me, trauma's power had turned me into stone, too. I became immovable and often shut others out without even realizing it. I would withdraw into myself, needing to be alone because only in solitude could I quiet the never-ending scanning of my environment for threats. This hyper-vigilance is a common symptom of PTSD, and it can make it difficult to relax or feel safe in any situation.

Yet, despite the challenges that come with trauma, it is possible to heal and overcome its effects. With the right support and resources, people who have experienced trauma can learn to manage their symptoms and live fulfilling lives. It takes time, patience, and a willingness to confront the past, but it is possible to move forward and find peace.

Trauma is a powerful force that can have far-reaching effects beyond the individual to whom it occurred. The story of Medusa is a tragic example of this. Medusa, who had no power to hurt Neptune or Minerva, punished anyone who came close to her. Her rage was blind and all-consuming, leaving her unable to distinguish between good and bad. To her, all men were evil, and all women were envious destroyers. As a result, the temple where she lived became full of innocent victims who were turned into stone by her curse. The area surrounding her lair was filled with stone statues of people who were entirely unable to comfort her, others, or themselves.

Unfortunately, I, too, have experienced the effects of trauma in my life. Like Medusa, I have turned away from those who tried to help me, refused their offers of friendship, and hurt them with my silence. The pain I experienced seemed too great to bear, and I did not want to burden others with it. But as I have grown and healed, I have come to realize that the isolation and distance I created only compounded my pain. It takes tremendous courage to confront one's own pain and seek help, but it is a necessary step toward healing and finding peace. I hope that by sharing my experience, I can encourage others who may be struggling to reach out and seek the support they need.

Trauma's true power is that it can overwhelm the body's central nervous system, altering how we process and recall memories. The potential is that we will remain a statue of stone for life. Dr. Van der Kolk wrote, "Trauma is not the story of something that happened back then." He adds, "It's the current imprint of that pain, horror, and fear living inside people."[8]

If trauma is to be transformed, we must take another valuable lesson from Medusa's story. Perseus, the son of Zeus, was given the quest to kill Medusa. He was warned not to look at her directly but to use his shield. Ironically, when Perseus beheaded Medusa, she was no longer bound by the trauma and gave birth to twins: Pegasus, the winged horse, and Chrysaor, of the golden blade.[9] In much the same way, it's not until we cut off the head of our trauma that new birth or healing can occur.

The abandonment of the familiar is a terrifying prospect for anyone who has lived through a traumatic event. We want to forget, not relive our trauma. Unlike Perseus, however, our goal is not to kill Medusa; she remains a victim, but rather, to kill the metaphor she represents, to destroy the trauma. For healing to occur, we must get close enough to our trauma to "behead" it, to take away its power to control us.

Our journeying companions are the "equivalent" of Perseus's reflecting shield. Only with a companion, a reflecting "shield," can we get close enough to our trauma, to take away its power, so that recovery can begin. I still cannot look at every one of my traumatic events; some of them remain acutely painful. I know that some of my early childhood trauma remains outside of my awareness.

Some years ago, as part of my military career, my wife and I lived in central Japan. There, I learned about Kintsugi,[10] the art of putting broken pottery pieces back together with gold as the bond. This type of art becomes a powerful metaphor for healing from trauma. Sometimes, in the process of repairing things that have been broken, we can create

Kinsugi

something more unique, beautiful, and resilient.

This notion is essential because I can never fully appreciate my new wholeness until I've realized, gathered, and bound my brokenness with the gold of God's mercy, grace, and forgiveness.

Chapter 2

MY "FAMILY"

Bent or broken is the family tree.
Each branch is a part of me.
This is my tree, and it's a big ol' tree.[11]
—Rein Perr

THE TYPE OF FAMILY YOU were raised in is crucial. It is the first setting where you learn who you are. Your family plays an important role in shaping your personality, beliefs, values, and attitudes. Are you loved or unloved? Is this new and strange place safe or unsafe? These are some of the questions that a child may ask themselves when growing up in a family. The foundational part of our identity becomes ingrained into us as values and life lessons are absorbed with

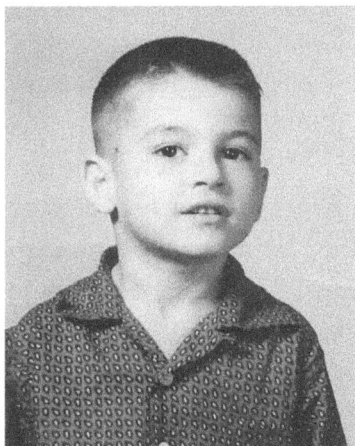

John's Kindergarten Picture

both positive and negative consequences. We accept those standards as our own, even though they may have been injected into us through an unstable and violent person. They affect how we view ourselves, how we treat others, and what we see as our purpose in life.

Growing up in a healthy family environment can provide a child with a sense of security, self-worth, and confidence. It can also teach them important life skills such as communication, problem-solving, and empathy. Unfortunately, not everyone gets to experience a healthy family environment. Some children grow up in abusive or neglectful households, which can have a lasting impact on their mental and emotional well-being.

In my case, I grew up in an unhealthy family environment. It was a place where love was scarce, and violence was prevalent. The constant fear and uncertainty made it difficult for me to form healthy relationships and trust others. However, I have learned to overcome these challenges and have become a stronger and more resilient person as a result.

The Mother I Wanted

In the TV show Leave It to Beaver, Barbara Billingsley portrayed the "perfect" mom, June Cleaver. She stayed home, helped with homework, was ready to talk anytime, and lovingly tucked her sons in at night. Her character was the epitome of a nurturing and caring mother, and it is no surprise that she became an icon of motherhood in American pop culture.

Unfortunately, that was not the type of mother I had. Growing up, my mother was distant and often absent. She didn't have much time for me or my brothers, and we often felt like we were on our own. Most likely, this was due to the trauma my mom experienced in her childhood. In 1947, at ten years of age, my mother and her older sister, Wrenella, who was thirteen at the time, contracted polio. They both became very sick and ended up in what was known as an "iron lung." An iron lung is a negative pressure ventilator whereby the entire body, except the person's head, is enclosed in a metal encasement. Polio was cruel to my mom but deadly to her sister. My mom came home, but her sister did not.

The experience of losing her sister at such a young age must have deeply affected my mother. Her childhood was marked by fear, anxiety, and uncertainty, and it is no wonder that she struggled to be the kind of mother that we needed. But despite her shortcomings, I know that my mother loved us in her own way and did the best she could with the cards she was dealt.

Reflecting on my mother's life, it is clear to me how her experiences shaped her as a person and as a mother. Her resilience and strength in the face of adversity are qualities that I deeply admire. Despite her hardships, my mother always did her best.

While I may not have had the June Cleaver-type of mother that I longed for, I am grateful for the lessons that my mother taught me, and for the person that she helped me become. I believe her sister's death forever marked my

Mom

mother's life. It was something she never talked about in depth. She only mentioned it once, and even then, her words conveyed that she felt that her parents would have rather had her die and her sister live. I can only imagine the survivor's guilt that she must have carried with her for so many years. Despite this, my mother never let her pain consume her. She always found a way to keep moving forward, no matter how difficult the road ahead. In many ways, my mother's strength and resilience have been a guiding light for me, and I will always be grateful for the person she was and the love she gave.

THE MOTHER I HAD

My mother was still a child at fifteen when she conceived my older brother, Steve. I was born when she was seventeen. Then, less than a year later, when she was a few months pregnant with my younger brother, Randy, my biological father, JR, divorced her.

Then, in 1955, just after my mom celebrated her nineteenth birthday, she went out on a date. My aunt told me that what began as an ordinary evening out turned into a nightmare. In the darkness, as she and her date sat in their parked car, they witnessed a "mob" murder. It seems that had they not reported it to the police, things might have been OK, but they did report it, and the mob found out.

The result changed the entire trajectory of my mom's life and, therefore, mine. As a kid, I remember seeing her in pain, both physically and mentally. She would often have trouble sleeping and would wake up with nightmares. Her once outgoing and bubbly personality was now replaced with anxiety and fear. No one I've talked to knows what happened to the man she was with, but what happened to Mom was crystal clear based on my aunt's description of her bruised and bloodied body. They found her, beat her, and left her for dead. I don't know how long it took for her to recover. My aunt said it was a miracle she survived. And yet, despite everything she went through, my mom never talked about it. She never mentioned the attack. She just tried to move forward and take care of her children the best she could. No one was ever prosecuted for what happened to her and that still bothers me to this day. But what I do know is that my mom was a survivor. She had been through so much and yet she never let it define her. She was one of the strongest people I knew and I am so grateful to have had her in my life.

Growing up, I had a skewed perception of the mob. In my childhood mind, they essentially only messed with others in the mob; they didn't want outsiders involved. So, if you got hurt by the mob, it was basically your fault. I used to wonder if that was the legacy of *The Naked City,* a TV show one of my mother's boyfriends watched religiously. I got the narrative from someplace, and it was a narrative that made me blame my mom for what happened that day. In essence, my very young brain could only imagine one narrative. I thought that the only way for my mom to witness a mob hit was to be a part of the mob. I remember thinking, "Mom, this wouldn't have happened if you hadn't been there." Looking back, I couldn't have been more wrong.

I now know that my perception of the mob was a simplified and erroneous one. The truth is that the mob is a complex and dangerous organization that preys on people regardless of their affiliation. My mom was just in the wrong place at the wrong time, and it was sheer luck that she managed to escape alive. That incident had a lasting impact on me, and it took me years to come to terms with the fact that my mom was not to blame. I learned that sometimes the world is a scary and unpredictable place, and bad things can happen to good people for no apparent reason. But I also learned that it is important to challenge our assumptions and seek the truth, even when it is uncomfortable.

The memories of our early childhood days are often hazy, but some moments leave an indelible mark on our psyche. One such memory for me is the time when my mother was recovering from her life-altering beating, and I was only fourteen months old. I have no recollection of where I was during that time, but I presume that I must have spent some time with an uncle or aunt. However, what I do remember vividly is the feeling of emptiness that engulfed me during my mother's absence. It was as if a part of me was missing, and I couldn't comprehend why my mother had left me.

Despite my tender age, I knew that I had a mother, and I would often whisper to myself, "I have a mommy." This thought gave me solace and hope that she would come back someday. I would eagerly look forward to the day when she would hold me in her arms. And she did come back. Her return filled my heart with joy and erased all the pain and anguish that I had endured during her absence.

Looking back, I realize that this experience taught me the power of hope and resilience. Even as a tiny child, I learned to hold on to the belief that things would get better, and they did. It is a lesson that has stayed with me throughout my life, and I am grateful for it.

Though I loved my mother, there were many times that I didn't like her very much. On my journey toward recovery, however, the narrative through which I view my mother has changed. I can now say, "Mom, I'm so sorry that you experienced this horrible event. You did not deserve this."

She was, in fact, like Medusa, an innocent victim. As a single mother, Mom did everything she could to make a living by working several jobs. She worked as a scantily clad roller-skating fast-food waitress by day and a bar waitress at night. That meant we three young boys, Steve, Randy, and I, were largely unsupervised. It seemed normal to be engaged in hours and hours of unchaperoned play.

One of the primary benefits of my journey toward recovery has been restoring some good memories of my mother. I have even been able to turn some of the black-and-white still photos in my mind into brief color video clips!

I was only five at the time, but I still remember watching Mom preparing for her twenty-first birthday party. As she put on her makeup, wearing a full-length white slip, she stood as an inspiring contrast of beauty in an otherwise dark and dismal bathroom. Even at a young age, with her dark, brown eyes, and wavy, raven-black hair styled like Marilyn Monroe's, I knew she was a knockout, the common lingo at the time. I was always proud to have her attend school events because she was so pretty.

A few other good memories have also returned, like how she often kissed my owies and boo-boos to make them feel better. Or how she made me a Halloween costume out of black plastic garbage bags so I would have something for trick or treat. She also helped with school projects whenever she could. Together, we would count the quarters she was usually given in tips, and I can even recall how she spent hours making items from plaster of Paris molds so my brothers and I could make some pocket money by selling them door to door. Who wouldn't want a plaster of Paris playing card symbol to sit on a shelf?

What you didn't want to do was make Mom mad! Whenever she came home from one of her jobs, she would invariably find a mess and "lose it." The only thing I knew for sure was that you'd better run fast when Mom got angry. She could go from zero to sixty miles per hour in a nanosecond! I made sure to cover my head because what she hit you with was always a matter of opportunity: a belt, stick, pot, pan, broom, or whatever else might be convenient. Most often, she preferred a hairbrush, a stiff-bristled one at that. However, it was never too bad because her actions were more nondirected fury than targeted harm. Although, the pinch under the arm would undeniably get my attention![12]

The Father I Wanted

I had never met my biological father until one day in August 1976, while on my honeymoon with Barbara. I'm sure I saw him as a baby, but I have no memory of him whatsoever. However, when I was five, or maybe six, I remember watching the Walt Disney movie *The Shaggy Dog*, starring Fred MacMurray and Annette Funicello.[13] Somehow, Fred MacMurray immediately became a father image to me. In this movie, as his son transformed back and forth into a dog, he unreservedly stood by him. That's what I imagined a father should do: give unconditional love and support.

Later, Fred MacMurray played a professor in the movie *The Absent-Minded Professor*.[14] I intentionally practiced being absent-minded for years, and perhaps that's why I still would love to be a professor. Also, as soon as it was legal to buy tobacco, I smoked a pipe just like his TV persona often did.

In the TV sitcom *My Three Sons*, Fred MacMurray played a widower with three sons.[15] Literally, in black and white, he demonstrated that it was possible to raise boys without violence. His character also clearly displayed how women were to be loved and respected.

Growing up, I didn't have a positive male role model in my life. My mom had a string of boyfriends who were either abusive or neglectful towards me and my siblings. It was a difficult and confusing time for me, and I longed for a father figure who was consistent, caring, and nonviolent.

That's why I turned to Fred MacMurray's characters in movies and TV shows. His portrayal of a father figure was so different from what I had experienced in real life. He was calm and level-headed and always had a solution to any problem.

Watching him on screen positively impacted my life in a big way. It showed me that you don't have to be violent or expressively angry to get things done or to discipline children. You can be kind, patient, and understanding while still being a strong and effective parent.

Even now, as an adult, I still look back on those characters and appreciate the impact they had on me. I am grateful for the positive

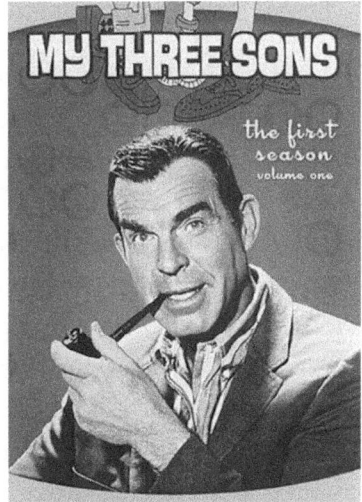

influence they had on my life and for the lessons they taught me about what a good father should be.

The "Father" I Had

A responsible man is someone who consistently makes choices that align with his values, even when it's difficult. He has a strong moral compass and doesn't do things he knows are wrong, nor does he blame others for his mistakes.

A reliable man understands the importance of hard work. He knows that the success of his family and his community depends on his ability to fulfill his role and protect their wellbeing.

A strong man is someone who knows how to keep his emotions in check. He understands that getting angry or upset doesn't solve the problem, so he calmly limits his reactions and thinks carefully before responding. He doesn't let his emotions control him, but rather uses his logic and reason to make the best decisions.

A committed man is someone who takes his relationships seriously. He never cheats on his partner, as he thinks of his affection as a full-time commitment. He values loyalty and honesty and always strives to maintain open and honest communication with his loved ones. He knows that a strong relationship requires effort and dedication, and he's willing to put in the work to make it last.

One of the men my mother brought into my life was the exact opposite of Fred MacMurray's image of a father figure. My mom's boyfriend, Eddie, was not a responsible, reliable, robust, or a committed man. I believe he was the perfect opposite of all the above statements: He was, and continues to be, the meanest man I ever knew.

Chapter 3

THE MEANEST MAN I EVER KNEW

EDDIE WAS ONE OF THE toughest men in a tough neighborhood and he took pride in his ability to intimidate others. Violence was a prevalent way to deal with problems. I remember the day when he threatened me, and I had to run away to avoid a physical altercation. His memory continued to haunt me for years, and I found myself constantly thinking about him and his violent ways.

Eddie

It wasn't until I turned eleven that I made a critical decision that changed my life forever. On that day, I deliberately decided to be a nonviolent person. I realized that violence only led to more problems and that it was not the solution to any conflict. I chose to take the high road and not follow Eddie's way of dealing with problems.

Since that day, I have tried my best to stay away from violence and to approach conflicts in a peaceful and rational manner. It hasn't always been easy, but I can now look back at my childhood and Eddie's memory without fear or regret.

No Refuge

Eddie was a police detective. He wasn't that large of a man; I guess he was about five feet, ten inches, but solid and robust. To an eight-year-old, he was huge but also menacing and unpredictable. His hair was cropped close, and he almost always wore a suit, tie, and short-brim fedora. With an ever-present cigarette hanging out of his mouth, he was a man to be obeyed: no-nonsense, no small talk, no discussion, no sense of humor, nothing. And hidden somewhere on him—his ankle, his back, or in a side holster—was his ever-present pistol, a Smith & Wesson .38 Special.

Eddie was a man of exquisite, random violence. Every time he appeared, he seemed to make it his mission in life to kick, hit, and verbally abuse my mother, brothers, and me.[16] That is why I wrote, "The meanest man I ever knew," on the back of his picture. Trying to hide from him was like trying to run from Superman, but this Superman was brutal.

Growing up in a household with an abusive parent is a nightmare that no child should ever have to endure. Unfortunately, I was one of those children who had to live through the constant fear and agony that came with it. I could always sense when Eddie was in a particularly bad mood, like a wild animal ready to pounce at any moment. It was like walking on eggshells all the time, never knowing when he would snap and lash out at us.

The physical abuse was the worst part. He didn't care what he used to hurt us, as long as it hurt. Belts, shoes, whatever was handy would do. And on the days when he didn't have an object to use, his bare hands were always there. I remember the sting of his hand slapping across my face, always leaving mark.

The psychological abuse was damaging too. The constant fear and anxiety that came with never knowing when the next attack would come was overwhelming. We were always on edge, waiting for the other shoe to drop. And even when he wasn't physically hurting us, his words and actions were always meant to belittle and control us.

Looking back, I know that Eddie thought he did a good job. He never killed us, after all. But the truth is, the scars he left on us will last a lifetime. No child should ever have to grow up feeling like they're constantly in danger. The sound of Eddie's car pulling into the driveway always made us boys run to hide. I can't remember when, but at some point, we must have all decided that only alone did we stand a chance of not being found. I would often scamper up the steep, creaky, narrow, and unevenly spaced stairs of our tiny garage apartment in hopes of escaping his blind, unreasonable, and explosive anger. Most days, however, he would find and beat me. There didn't need to be a reason.[17]

To this day, I still don't know where my brothers hid. Strangely, it was as if they weren't even there. I only have a few memories of my brothers in them. I wasn't even present; how could they be?

A Hiding Place

When there is no security in the home, there is no refuge. Even though I didn't believe there was a God, I often found myself appealing to Him for protection. After one ferocious beating, I could not stop sobbing; I tried to stop but couldn't. With each escaping sob, Eddie became increasingly angry and beat me even harder. I was confused because I felt nothing. No tears were coming from my eyes, but I could not stop sobbing. Mom stood by, as she often did, helplessly crying. That day, I begged God to reach down from His far-off heaven and give me a haven, a refuge. It wasn't long after, I believe, that God answered my request.

It was my job to gather the laundry from the clothes hamper twice a week. I was not fond of this chore because the hamper was in the small space below the stairs. Getting the clothes out often meant facing giant tree cockroaches or rats. Then, there was always the ever-present, unpleasant stink of urine. I can only assume all of us boys still wet bed; I know I did until I was thirteen. My mother said that the laundry always "stunk to high heaven."

However, one day, while gathering the laundry, I heard Eddie's car pull into the driveway. Without thinking, I quickly jumped into that clothes hamper and rolled up into a fetal position. It was as if I had entered a different world; I could hear my heart beating, not simply the pounding but the actual sound of it hammering in my chest. I was as quiet as possible, keeping my mouth open wide to allow the air to flow freely into my lungs. I didn't dare take a deep breath; Eddie might hear.

As usual, Eddie came through the entire house cursing and screaming, looking for Mom but eager to find someone to take his anger out on. He threatened us. "If you don't come out, I'll knock you into next week." He checked everywhere: opening and slamming doors in the kitchen, bathroom, closets, and looking under beds. I was sure he would find me, but he didn't. This time, he gave up and went away. He never thought to look in the dirty clothes hamper!

I wish there were some way to share with you the profound joy I felt. A miracle had just happened; I hid, and Eddie did not find me! God had given me a sanctuary, a refuge. My mom always said that the hamper stunk to high heaven. To this day, I believe that the dirty clothes hamper was not only heaven sent but heaven scent!

WAKE-UP CALL

When you were growing up, did you ever have the unhappy experience of putting your finger into a light socket? It makes your hair stand up. I knew some kids who did it for fun, but not me, that's for sure.

Do you know what a cattle prod is? It is a battery-operated device designed to move cows wherever you want them to go by delivering a powerful shock between two electrodes. Sadly, in the 1960s and before, some police used them for crowd control.[18]

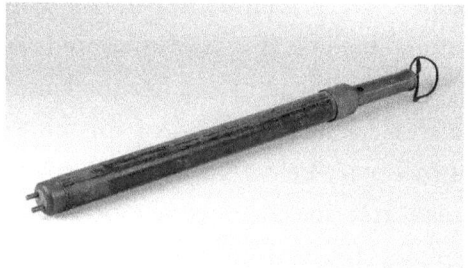

I'll never forget the first time, unfortunately, the first of many, when Eddie woke me up with a jolt. He pressed those two electrodes of a cattle prod to the soles of my bare feet. He thought it was humorous, but it was certainly not for me. To this day, I cannot sleep if my feet are uncovered. Even the slightest exposure will suddenly wake me up for fear of exposing my feet to his sadism.

In my fifties, I tried conducting exposure therapy[19] on myself. Exposure therapy was developed to help people confront their fears. I knew I didn't need a sheet to cover my feet in my own home, so for a few months, I tried various levels of exposure therapy. After the third month, I felt the therapy was somewhat successful because I could fall asleep with my feet uncovered. However, the slightest touch of anything would still cause me to wake up in fear.

Then I asked myself a simple question. "Why not just keep my feet covered?" If a mere sheet over my feet allowed me to sleep soundly through the night, why not use one? It didn't hurt me; it didn't hurt anyone else. So, I stopped the exposure therapy and, over a decade later, I sleep soundly with my feet safely tucked under a sheet.

Under the Truck

As a police officer, Eddie had access to prisoners and would often bring home someone from the prison to help him with a house he was building; I suppose it was something like a work-release program. Located on a five-acre unworked piece of land, I remember a large wooden platform, maybe thirty feet by twenty feet, probably ten feet tall, and covered with black plastic.

Sometimes, Mom and we boys would go out to the land with them. One night, because it was sprinkling a little, Mom and Eddie were sleeping in the truck's cab while we three boys were sleeping underneath it; without blankets or anything else, all we had on was our underwear. The South can be warm like that.

I remember waking up in the middle of the night to something scratching on my shirtless back. At first, I thought I was dreaming, but the sensation persisted. It was odd, so I raised up as much as possible and looked down. I couldn't believe what I saw! Three scorpions were running around in a circle, chasing each other on the ground. I froze, not wanting to make any sudden movements in case they decided to attack me. Although I was terrified, I kept my eyes on them, watching their every move.

Suddenly, one of them stopped and raised its tail, ready to strike. I knew I had to act fast. Without thinking, I hit my head on the muffler as I scampered out from under the truck and started beating on the cab door, shouting, "Let me in! Let me in! Let me in!" I could feel my heart pounding in my chest as I waited for someone to open the door. It seemed like an eternity before I heard the click of the lock, and the door swung open. I stumbled into the cab, gasping for air and shaking with fear.

From that day on, I always made sure to check my surroundings before going to sleep, especially if I was out camping in the wilderness. It was a lesson learned the hard way, but one that I would never forget. Mom and Eddie were none too pleased, but I was terrified and willing to risk whatever happened. Somehow, they managed to clear out the back of the truck, and I finally went back to sleep. As in many other episodes, I can't remember what happened before or after or where Steve and Randy were; in my mind, I was the only one there.

ALL ABOARD THE GUILT TRAIN

I unhappily remember when, one day, Eddie stormed into our apartment and said, "I hope you boys are proud of yourselves. You're the reason your mom's in the hospital."

Lining us up, he continued his rampage with every swear word and expletive known at the time. Isn't it odd? Eddie was the one who physically beat my mother into unconsciousness, where she lay in her waste for several days. He was the one who caused the injuries that put her in the hospital. I had nothing to do with it, but as sure as the sun would rise tomorrow, I was the one who felt guilty.

My ten-year-old mind knew that Eddie's words were not true. He beat my mom frequently, and I often heard her screams at night. Blaming us for what he did? If we'd been better kids, he wouldn't have beat her? I knew what he was saying wasn't true; he was a liar, but what I knew and felt were two entirely different things.

Guilt is funny; I couldn't even share it with my brothers. Like many raised with cruel or insensitive adults, I believed it was all my fault. Though I don't remember how my mother got to the hospital, I do remember trying to wake her up; everything else was blank. The thought of harming the only person who gave me a sense of value was overwhelming. Yet I, not he, was the one reduced to a bit of wound-up guilt, hardly able to breathe.

DANGLING BY A THREAD

Regrettably, you are never fully prepared for what might trigger memories of your childhood traumas. It wasn't until a tragic day in 2003 that I remembered one of those events. Being tied and hung upside down is one of the many things Eddie would do to me. I remember how he would bind my hands and feet together and dangle me upside down from a swing set. He seemed to get great glee from seeing how far he could drop me before my head hit the ground. Fortunately, I usually managed to roll my head to the side so my shoulder would hit the ground first.

Most people don't know that there's a stretch of road in front of the United States Air Force Academy in Colorado Springs, Colorado, that is controlled by the Academy Security Forces. Sadly, in 2003, there was a fourteen-car pileup on that stretch of road. As the chaplain for the Security Forces, the commander called and asked me to meet him at the accident site.

It was a very tragic scene. A semitruck driver had to swerve into the median to avoid plowing into several cars. His action most likely saved many lives; however, in the process, his tractor-trailer truck ran directly over a little family car that had also diverted into that same median. I immediately went up to the driver of the tractor-trailer truck and found him frozen to the wheel, looking straight ahead. Most likely, his mind had distanced itself from what had just happened. He was mentally in another place and did not appear to hear me at all.

I then headed down to the car that the semi had run over. What I saw was heartbreaking. A seven- or eight-year-old girl's body was hanging upside down, dangling by her seat belt. This young girl had been killed instantly, but since only the coroner could move the body, she had to remain suspended until they arrived.

It was at that very moment that I recalled the trauma of being tied and hung upside down by Eddie. As the little girl's body could easily be seen from the road, until the coroner arrived, we formed a circle around her to offer what dignity we could. The image of that little girl dangling from her seat belt, like many traumatic events in my childhood, will be forever etched in my mind.

Foul Play

My childhood was marked by constant moving from one place to another. That context continues to obscure my search for the past. So, when my mom witnessed yet another murder, Eddie swiftly whisked us away to a remote one-room stone house far from town. There, we had to remain hidden for several months.

During that time, there stood an old shed in the middle of the abandoned lot, teeming with yellow jackets — those small, cantankerous predator wasps. They seemed to have taken over the place, and their buzzing could be heard from quite some distance away. One day, while exploring the area, I stumbled upon the shed and saw the largest nest I'd ever seen. It was hanging from the ceiling, a menacing sight that I couldn't ignore.

I stood there, transfixed, fascinated by the sheer size of the nest. But then, a thought crossed my mind, and I decided to test my aim. I picked up a medium-sized rock, took a deep breath, and threw it at the nest. However, my pitching skills were lacking, and my first attempt missed the target, managing only to rile up the swarm.

Undeterred, I picked up another rock and, this time, scored a direct hit. The rock hit the nest with a loud thud, and I could hear the angry buzz of the yellow jackets growing louder. Suddenly, they were everywhere, swarming around me, attacking me from all directions. I tried to run, but it was too late. They had already started stinging me.

Little did I know, this would lead to a frenzy of over twenty painful stings. The pain was excruciating. Having been stung on both eyelids, my eyes instantly swelled shut, and I was afraid that I had been blinded. I fell as I tried to run into the house and there I lay, helpless and in pain, until someone found me and took me to the hospital.

It took me several days to recover from the ordeal, and during that time, I had a lot of time to reflect. I learned a valuable lesson: never mess with the yellow jackets. I realized that I had been careless and had not taken the necessary precautions to protect myself. From that day forward, I made sure to always wear protective clothing while outdoors, and I made sure to keep a safe distance from any potential hives.

A few days later, while my grandparents were playing their favorite game of dominoes, I mustered all my strength and managed to crack open one of my eyelids. To my sheer delight, I succeeded, and through the narrow slits, I realized I wasn't blind! Overjoyed, I briefly interrupted their dominoes match, happily racing around the house with my newfound ability to see. Much like, after I received my first pair of glasses while serving in the army, when I stepped outside and was struck by the revelation that trees had individual leaves on them!

My journey toward recovery continues to be filled with similar breathtaking moments along the way. Some days are tougher than others, but I am learning to take it one step at a time. Every small victory gives me hope and keeps me motivated to keep going. I am grateful for the support I have received from my loved ones and healthcare professionals who have been with me every step of the way. Though the journey may be long and challenging, I am determined to stay strong and keep moving forward.

Chapter 4

HOME ALONE

Loneliness expresses the pain of being alone
and solitude expresses the glory of being alone.[20]
—Paul Tillich

LEAVING A CHILD AT HOME ALONE FOR THE FIRST
time can be a difficult decision for any parent. It's a big step for both the
child and the parent. However, my mother never seemed to struggle
with that decision. She would leave us at home whenever she wanted to,
without any hesitation. Most experts recommend that parents hold off
on letting their children stay alone overnight until they are in their late
teens. However, I had already left home for good at the age of fifteen. Was
it because I had been left alone for much of my life? I can't say for sure. But
sometimes I wonder if my early independence was a result of my mother's
approach to leaving us alone.

A Puppy, a Nurse, and a Long Night

The road was busy, but I seemed to be invisible. I just sat on the curb
crying and sobbing, alone and cold in the darkness. I looked intently into
the window of each approaching car, searching for my mother's face. I was
inconsolable and, more than anything, desperately needed someone to
care for me or simply to stop and ask if I needed help.

About a month earlier, I was given a puppy. I don't know whether
Mom got him for me, or if I had just found him on the side of the road. He
was tiny, black, furry, and full of bounce and vigor. It was summer, so my

days were filled with endlessly playing with him and he rapidly became my closest friend. In naming him Bourbon, some of my background will be telling, but to me, his name was as innocent and as pure as the driven snow.

One night, as I fell asleep, I felt overcome with a desire to tell my mother how much I loved her, so I said, "Mommy, I love you as much as I love Bourbon."

"Gee, thanks," she responded.

Her answer hurt and confused me. I get it now; no one wants to be compared to a dog, even if it is a cute puppy. I fear I hurt my mom in an immature moment but with childlike innocence. Apparently, she didn't understand that I was paying her the highest compliment I knew how to, or she perhaps didn't understand how much I loved her.

Later that week, Bourbon and I were running around outside chasing each other. I can't remember whether I ran into the house to get water or go to the bathroom, but when I returned, an attractive young woman was standing there on the sidewalk. She wore a beautiful white dress with white shoes and a little white hat: a nurse's outfit. Tears were streaming down her face.

She saw me and asked, almost sobbing, "Little boy, do you know who owns this dog?"

That's when I saw Bourbon lying dead on the street. She continued. "I was driving home when he ran into the street, and I couldn't stop."

Something inside me locked up. I felt like I had been hit, but there was no pain, only I don't know what it was—simultaneously numb and not numb. On the one hand, I felt like my world was coming apart, but on the other hand, I said, "I don't know. I'll go ask."

Then I turned and ran to the house. A torrent of grief overwhelmed me when I got around the corner, and I was undone. I fell to the ground and cried as hard as I ever remember. All I wanted was my mommy, but as usual, she wasn't home.

Through my years of counseling training, I have learned how important it is to be present with myself and others; being present[21] means being fully conscious of the moment and free from the noise of internal dialogue. After all these years, I believe now that if I had been

25

able to be present with that nurse, she could have brought me a measure of comfort. She certainly felt horrible about running over Bourbon. I imagine she would have knelt, taken me into her arms, and told me how sorry she was. Perhaps our tears would have mingled. Sadly, that idea will forever remain a fantasy.

The option of being present with the nurse, or anyone, had already been taken from me; Eddie, I suppose, had ripped that ability from my heart with his frequent words of, "Don't you cry, or I'll give you something to cry about."

He beat us if we cried, if we lost a fight, or if he felt disrespected. Withdrawing internally, I would try not to cry because it wasn't worth the double pain. I learned how to cry silently; without tears, I could only be present or in the moment when I was alone.

After the nurse had left, I began my vigil on the curb, waiting for my mom to return. Time passed very slowly. As a nine-year-old, I needed her to pick me up, comfort me, and tell me everything would be all right. She was the only person in my young world with whom I could still feel secure.

However, I just sat there on the curb, tears flowing down my face, my head in my hands, visibly and vocally sobbing, begging for someone driving down Cullen Street to see me. All I wanted was for someone to stop, get out of their car, come over to me, and ask, "What happened?" How can I help?" "How can I make it better?" "Can I wait with you until your mother returns?" "Do you need a doctor?" However, no one stopped.

Throughout my childhood, I frequently had awful headaches; that night, my headache was dreadful. Sometimes, when I would get one, I couldn't even stand the sound of people walking in another room. I had to be in total darkness, with a pillow wrapped around my head, until I cried myself to sleep. But there was no pillow for me that evening, no silence, only the passing of cars and the black of night. I knew my mother could make the pain disappear if she only came. Only, she never came that night. The last thing I recall was crying myself to sleep.

I internalized that loss, pushed it out of my mind, and never experienced any closure until, while a chaplain in the United States military, I was asked to conduct a funeral for a military working dog. When a military dog dies, their owner experiences a substantial emotional injury. The bond between a working dog and its partner is distinctive; the dog may have even saved their life.

My first thought was as thoughtless as most people would have. A funeral? For a dog? However, to comfort those who were grieving, I decided to conduct the funeral and it ended up being far more meaningful than I ever thought.

While performing the service, my mind unexpectedly went back to the night I lost Bourbon and, as my tears mixed with those in attendance, I was able to conduct a funeral in my mind for my little puppy, Bourbon. As we grieved together, at least in part, I was finally able to say goodbye to my little friend.

OF BONFIRES AND MARBLES

On one occasion, when we had been alone again for at least three or four days, Eddie showed up and lined us up like we were in an interrogation room. One by one, and not in a kind way, he demanded to know where our mom was. I remember being terrified as he demanded answers to his questions about who mom was with, when we saw her last, where she went, and on and on. I don't know if he was drunk, but I knew he was unstable and could go off anytime. Thankfully, this time, he did not turn his anger on us.

As he became increasingly agitated, Eddie started pulling all of Mom's things out of the dressers and closets and dumping them onto the floor. He relished tearing into Mom's costume jewelry and the beads flew everywhere. Living in an apartment above a garage, he stormed over to the window, opened it, and tossed everything to the yard below. Then he went outside, created a huge pile, and lit it all on fire.

What were we boys doing as we watched our mother's belongings being used as a bonfire? Randy and I played marbles with the beads from Mom's costume jewelry. What else could we do?

SHOWING OFF

One day, we three boys had somehow procured a bow and arrow set. While playing in the street outside our apartment building, and not being the sharpest pencils in the box, we thought it would be fun to shoot them straight into the air and dodge them as they came down.

It seems striking now that no adults told us to stop because it was dangerous. Yet no one did, either because they did not know what we were doing or did not care. Anyway, one of the arrows I shot into the air went awry and landed on the roof of a house across from our apartment building.

Now, in my estimation, the house it landed on was really uptown because it had a swamp cooler! Swamp coolers are technically evaporative coolers. They pass outdoor air over water-saturated pads, and when the water evaporates, they can substantially reduce the air temperature inside the home. Though preferable to the Texas summer heat, the humidity it created made everything damp.

Being light, nimble, and quick, I swiftly scrambled onto their swamp cooler to get to the roof. Once there, I grabbed the arrow and, given that several kids were watching, with great pomp and circumstance threw it down to the ground, sticking the pointy end into the dirt.

The roof I fell off of 58 years later!

Unfortunately, as I was climbing down, my bare feet slipped on the moisture dripping off the swamp cooler, and I fell. In an instant, I found myself hanging upside down. I didn't know how or why I hadn't fallen to the ground; it felt like something had hit my knee with great force, more like a punch than anything else. I looked up to try to figure out what had happened. Then I saw it! My knee was hanging on one of the swamp cooler bolts! Somehow, I lifted myself up, pulled my knee off the bolt, and dropped to the ground.

It didn't hurt at first, but I began screaming and hollering, "I'm gonna die! I'm gonna die!" when I saw all the blood coming out of the gaping wound! A neighborhood girl found a sheet and wrapped my leg tight while my brother called Mom from one of the neighbors' houses. Mom asked to talk to me, but I was so distraught that she kept saying, "Put your brother back on the phone! Put your brother back on the phone!"

When Mom arrived, she drove me back to the Toy House, where she worked. As I was sitting in the car, a man walked up to the window, and Mom, ignoring my vigorous protestations to leave it alone, unwrapped my knee; the man took one look at it and said, "Yeah, you're going to have to take him to the hospital." Soon, my knee was stitched up, but I was told to stay off my leg for a while, something I know must have been torture for both my mother and me.

That was my first official introduction to the next man in my mom's life. He seemed nice enough; I first saw him as somewhat of a savior. He was very tall, powerful, and looked like the sort of man who could handle Eddie. However, I knew Eddie was mean, armed, and not afraid to hurt someone. I didn't know if this man had these skills, but he seemed like one who might. Little did I know that he could be almost as violent as Eddie but, thankfully, not nearly as unstable.

> ## Fret not yourself because of evildoers;
> ## be not envious of wrongdoers!
> ## For they will soon fade like the grass
> ## and wither like the green herb.
> ### - Psalm 37:1, 2b (ESV)

Chapter 5

LIFE LESSONS

Your life experiences are only as powerful
as your ability to transform them into life lessons.[22]
—Cleo Wade

A LIFE LESSON IS JUST WHAT IT SOUNDS LIKE—A
lesson you learn from your life experiences. Based on the idea of learning
from your mistakes, these lessons could be described as defining moments
that are remembered and lead to an opportunity for growth. I certainly
remember the following memories of mine. Were they beneficial to me?
Did they lead to an opportunity for growth? In some ways, yes, but I'm
convinced that most of the lessons I learned could have been achieved
differently.

Thou Shalt Not Steal

I was mighty proud when I learned to ride a bicycle around ten! As
communal property within the large apartment complex we lived in, that
bike was an absolute nightmare; it was too big for me, with no fenders,
crooked handlebars, and only one pedal. However, just down the road
from the complex was a gas station where I would often find a couple of
older men just sitting and fixing bicycles. It was fun to be around them, no
violence, no drama. Somehow, they got that bike set and ready for riding.

One day, while riding around, I met some other boys who lived in the
area. One of them showed me his cap gun, not the kind that used the red
paper cap roll but the sophisticated little plastic eight-shooter.

"Man, that's so cool! Where'd you get it?" I asked.

"I stole it," he replied.

"Stole it?" I responded in shock. "Where'd you steal it from?"

"There." He said as he pointed to the neighborhood corner market down the street.

"No kidding?" I said, "You just went in and picked it up?"

"Yep, just went in, picked it up, put it under my shirt, and walked out. It was easy."

So not to be outdone, scrawny, little, barefooted me, in shorts and wearing a T-shirt that was way too tight, walked down to that store. Confidently, I went in and roamed around for a bit. I thought I looked completely innocent but I'm sure to anyone around I must have appeared guilty.

I couldn't find the little gun, but I saw something else I liked: little rubber snakes, a package full of them. So, I looked around as sneakily as possible and slipped the package under my too-tight T-shirt. Then I stealthily approached the exit with my back to the person at the counter.

However, as I opened the door to leave, I heard the man behind the counter say, "Hey, boy, get back here."

I thought about bolting, but some adults were close by, and I knew they could quickly grab me, so I didn't and went back in.

"What do you have under your shirt?" he asked.

"Nothing," I replied.

"I can see something under your T-shirt, you know," he said.

At that point, I knew I had been caught. So, I pulled the snakes out from under my T-shirt and handed them over.

I was confused with what he said next. "You know, I'm gonna tell your dad."

Somehow, the store clerk knew Eddie. He knew him and called him my "dad." Sometimes, we called Eddie "Pop," but he sure wasn't my dad. The store clerk got on the phone, and it wasn't long before Eddie showed up.

When we returned to our little apartment, Eddie took me into the bedroom and made me remove all my clothes, underwear, and everything. After making me stretch out on the bed, face down, arms forward, and legs spread out, he took off his belt and used it, buckle end to the flesh, to beat the living daylights out of me. Yeah, that's the only way to put it. He beat every piece of my skin, from the top of my head, down my arms, and to the bottom of my feet.

That anything good could come from that beating, some may say, is ironic. I believe the cost of that good was far too high. I'll let you be the judge. But I'll tell you what. I never stole again.

Eddie taught me other things as well. You would think I wouldn't want to be anywhere near that man, but I found that my odds of being his target were lessened if I was helpful. Sometimes, he would let me ride with him in his unmarked squad car. Other times, he would park far from a scene of interest and have me get out to peer into a window or between some cracks in a door. My job was to listen to what was happening and report everything I had heard or seen back to him.

It's funny that events like that seem so natural when you're young, but as you grow up, you realize they are also the source of so much pain.

Always Flush the Toilet

I don't know who she was. Just some woman, not a babysitter, but somehow familiar. I don't think she was family, but I was in her home for some reason. I don't know how old I was; I could only guess I was somewhere between diapers and being fully potty trained.

At least I had used the toilet; some credit should be given where credit is due, but no, I had not flushed. She grabbed me by my arm and started screeching, more like a banshee than a person. Dragging me into the bathroom, she bellowed, "Look at that! Look at that, you little shit!" Then she stuck my head into the toilet.

I thought I was going to drown! Pulling my head out of the toilet momentarily, she loudly called me horrible names and demanded, "If you're not going to flush, then you're going to eat it! Eat it! Eat it!" She then shoved my head back into the toilet.

I tried to comply but, with all her shaking and dunking, eating my feces was impossible. Somehow, after I was able to take a couple of bites,

I remember involuntarily throwing up. What didn't land in the toilet got spewed on the seat and the floor.

Violently flinging me backward against the wall, she continued her tirade with swear words and hateful words that are not proper to repeat. As she stormed out of the bathroom she screamed, "You disgust me!" I was left whimpering alone with my confused tears and sick stomach. I don't recall that lady outside that event, and for that, I am grateful.

That one occurrence is why when I joined the army and a drill sergeant was dressing me down for some reason, all I could do was laugh. I had been physically beaten and emotionally abused for most of my life; what could he do to me? Thankfully, I wasn't the first broken adolescent man the army had to deal with. Military life had the extraordinary ability to offer me the structure and consistency I desperately needed. For that, I am eternally grateful.

Eggs over Easy

My brothers and I were accustomed to being alone. We were perfectly capable of fending for ourselves, right? Well, regrettably, it was not always perfect.

One time, I was hungry and wanted to eat some eggs. I loved eggs over easy but didn't want to flip them, so, I added enough grease to the pan to cover them completely. Unfortunately, some of the oil ran over the side and quickly caught on fire. Being the bright, intelligent, young boy I was, I carefully carried the burning cast iron skillet to the sink and stuck it under the faucet.

As I now know, this was a huge mistake! The water only made it worse. Flames shot out, and I dropped the skillet! As the burning oil poured down my leg onto my right foot, some exposed mesh backing on the kitchen walls erupted into flames.

I began running around screaming in pain at the top of my lungs like a chicken with its head cut off. When my brothers heard the commotion, they rushed in and managed to stop the fire by dosing everything with water and swatting the flames with towels or whatever else they could get their hands on.

I don't remember much that happened after, only the excruciating pain of my burns. At any rate, you get the point; we boys were mainly self-sufficient, but not entirely. I'm sure that allowing young boys home alone at our ages would not pass the Child Protection Service (CPS) test these days; sometimes, I wish CPS had been around back then.

BECOMING A MAN

Early one morning, one of my stepfathers woke me up saying, "Come with me, boy. Today, I'm going to make you into a man."

Apparently, he thought that being able to kill an animal for a purpose wasn't good enough to change boys into men; you had to do it up close; you had to relish it. I had often witnessed him purposely run over dogs and cats on the side of the road. That was hard for me to watch, even harder to feel the physicality of it, but it didn't hurt that much because I didn't know those animals; I never had to see the pain in their owners' faces.

On the farm we were living on at the time, we raised pigs. I remember picking up 55-gallon barrels of food scraps leftover from local area restaurants because it was the perfect slop mix to feed the pigs. Because of the pigs, though, there were also a lot of disgusting Wharf rats. The fact is, the first time I saw the rats down at the barn, they were so big I thought they were little dogs. I'll tell you; I didn't mind killing those rats. The rats even dug so many tunnels under the barn that it ultimately collapsed. There was also nothing unusual about killing the wild dogs on a farm; after seeing what a pack of dogs can do to the milk cow udders, you don't hesitate to shoot.

As we stood outside, he pointed into the distance to the stray dog I had recently befriended. My stepfather whistled to bring it close to us. As the dog approached, it was so happy his entire body shook as his tail wagged. That's when I felt my stepfather put a large pipe wrench into my hand and say, "When that dog gets close enough, you wump him upside the head and kill it, you hear."

That morning, I was being asked to kill not a wild dog, not a dog that had gotten after the pigs or cows or chickens, but a dog that had most likely just been abandoned on the side of the road. I couldn't do it. I desperately wanted his approval, but I just couldn't do it. His words that followed my refusal still ring in my memory. As he cursed, he told me that I was so stupid that I'd be dead before I was thirty.

The dog must have picked up on my anxiety because he moved off a little distance. Unable to lure him closer, my stepfather picked up his 30/06 rifle and unceremoniously shot him. It must have been a direct hit to the chest because, before the dog crumpled to the ground, I distinctly heard the air propel forcibly out of his lungs, '*pfffhhhht.*'

It wasn't long after that experience that my actual pet sheepdog, Pepper, disappeared. I was in a lot of grief; both the stray dog and Pepper were gone. My mother later told me that my stepfather had killed Pepper.

My hatred for that stepfather was sealed, my desire to get away was complete. At that moment, I knew I would rather be on my own, so, in some way, I did become a man that day.

Poverty

You have probably guessed by now that I grew up poor. I don't say that to elicit sympathy; we enjoyed life as well as anyone. I never thought of us as being poor, inferior, or different. Many times, because our only clothes were on our backs, my mom would make us sit in the back of the car naked as she went into a laundromat to wash our clothes, including our underwear.

I do, however, remember when I felt something akin to jealousy, although at the time it was closer to wonder. One of the moms in the neighborhood invited me into her house for some lemonade, and when I walked in, I saw a piano against the wall. On the other wall was a color TV. I was awestruck. A piano? A color TV? In a home? That these could be privately owned was amazing to me. I had only seen a piano at school.

Whenever we moved to a new area, I fondly remember the neighborhood welcome wagon. Someone would always bring us several bags of groceries. I don't know who arranged it, but it was the best, and what would we have done without the government cheese, peanut butter, and rice programs?

In one of my seminary classes, I recently took an exercise from Peggy McIntosh's "Privilege Walk Exercise."[23] Throughout the Privilege Walk, statements are read by a facilitator and the participants are asked to take a step forward or backward based on their responses. This activity forces participants to confront how society naturally privileges some individuals over others.

I scored a negative nine; only one person scored one step lower than me. The class members looked at me dubiously. I'm sure their minds were asking questions like, "How is that possible? You have four master's degrees and a doctorate; you could never honestly score a negative nine."

But I did! It was not a score I wanted, but it was the score I got. This is another proof that miracles do exist. Thanks to God, all things are indeed possible!

WITH GOD,
ALL THINGS ARE *possible*

MATTHEW 19:26

Chapter 6

MY FRIEND

A good friend is like a four-leaf clover:
hard to find and lucky to have.[24]
—Jenna Evans Welch

ISN'T IT AMAZING HOW SPECIFIC IMAGES CAN stick in your mind? Frozen there in perfect clarity? Charlie's 1956 yellow and white Chevrolet is one such image, as is a young girl named Melinda.

My Friend Lost

My mom's new boyfriend had a cool 1956 Chevy. One night, after we all went to a drive-in movie, my childhood was once more uprooted. Returning late to our apartment, and because I really had to pee, I immediately hopped out and ran up the steps. I don't know whether it was a night light or just the faint glow from our TV, but as I neared the door, I could see through the sheer curtains covering our living room window that Eddie was inside, seated in the reclining chair, facing the door, eyes closed, with his service shotgun across his chest.

Instantaneously, I knew we were in trouble! Quickly, I ran back down the stairs, knowing I needed to alert everyone about the situation. Shouting in a panicked whisper, I said, "Mom, Mom, he's gonna kill us. He's got the shotgun!"

Ordinarily, one would think that a mother would respond, "Now Johnny, stop it. You're just being silly; nobody will do anything."

But she didn't say that; that's not what happened. What did happen was that all of us quickly piled back into the Chevy and took off. My older brother had already started his Sunday morning paper route. After we found him, he was forced to abandon his new bike, recently purchased with his paper route money, on the side of the road.

Then we all drove five hours away to where our grandparents lived. Mom was confident that Eddie would soon be close behind, so, it wasn't long before we continued her boyfriend's family home in Georgia. That night ended Eddie's reign of fear and terror in my life.

In the 1980s, while a student at seminary, my wife, daughters, and I took a trip to see if I could find that old childhood apartment complex. We did find it, but it was closed and abandoned. In 2021, Barbara and I returned for another look, but by then, that apartment complex had been demolished; I only wish the memories of that night could be as well.

My Friend Found

Once again, I had been forced to leave all my few belongings behind. But the most enduring pain was never being able to say goodbye to my only friend, Melinda. Finding someone I could connect with was rare, but we did connect. We were the same age, and she was so cute. We even held hands several times, but we mostly spent time together playing as any other ten-year-old kids would do.

I don't remember the first time I met her, but I'll never forget the night I left her. Suffice it to say that Melinda, or my representation of Melinda, has been with me for over half a century. Although I certainly wouldn't have thought of it this way back then, my connection with Melinda proved that I was not irredeemably broken; I could make a meaningful connection with someone.

Recently, on my journey toward recovery, I recalled that it was Melinda's swamp cooler that I fell from. She was the girl who had wrapped my bloody knee in a sheet! It became clear that to recover from some of my childhood trauma, I needed to say goodbye to Melinda so that I could say hello to other things in my life. At the very least, I needed to gain some notion of closure, but after fifty-seven years, would it be possible to find her and say goodbye?

Over the past forty-five years, to help give my life a more extensive foundation, I've become quite adept at genealogy research. So, I went to work on trying to find the Melinda of my past. Nothing followed nothing, which followed nothing. Then out of the blue, I remembered her last name! More research allowed me to find a family with her last name, but they were longtime residents of another city. Still, I wondered if there was a possibility that they had ever lived where I had.

After more internet research, I found a possible Melinda with a different last name. Should I take the chance? Now that I had an actual name to contact, the abstract nature of the pursuit became very concrete. What if she thought I was a crazy person?

Thankfully, reason took over, and I said to myself, "You've waited fifty-seven years to do this; do it and let the chips fall where they may." However, I wasn't confident enough to call, so I texted.

"Hi, Melinda. Sorry to bother you. My name is John, and I'm looking for a Melinda I knew in 1965 or 1966 when I was ten years old and lived in Houston. Any possibility that was you? Thanks."

To my great amazement, she soon responded, "Maybe. We moved from Houston in 1966."

I wrote, "Seriously? I lived off Old Spanish Trail. Do you remember a boy who just disappeared? I also cut my knee."

She replied, "Yes. You cut your knee on our house fan. How did you get my number?"

It was her! I was stunned, surprised, giddy, and afraid all at once. I answered her question with another text. "I was looking on Ancestry.com for your name and then did an internet search, and your number popped up. I have wanted to say goodbye to you for fifty-seven years! We left in the middle of the night because of a violent family abuse situation, and I never got to say goodbye. That night marked a turning point in my life that, unknown to you, made you an indelible part of my memory. After leaving home, I've had a wonderful life, but I think finally saying goodbye to you will open up my childhood for me. I hope this doesn't sound too strange. I apologize if it does."

Her response was "No. I always wondered what had happened. My blessings to you!"

I responded, "Thank you!"

To which she wrote, "Take care, my friend."

It's impossible to describe my feelings here. My first thoughts must have been similar to Pinocchio's. "I'm a real boy!" Someone had validated that not only were my memories real but that I had also been her friend.

I do not speak much of my childhood. How do you share what others may think to be tainted, exaggerated, or made up? Melinda's validation of an event in my life was, and remains to this day, as refreshing as a cool drink on a 130-degree day while deployed in the desert: impossible to describe but even more so to forget.

Like cold water
to a thirsty soul,
so is good news from
a far country.

Proverbs 25:25 (ESV)

Chapter 7

MEMORIES RECOVERED

What's left when we leave: photos, souvenirs, empty clothes?
Yes, but are those what matter? No, it's the stories behind them.
Stories live forever, but only if you tell them.
—Bud Vogel[25]

IN THE 1970S, I FLEW A SMALL PLANE FOR A painting company in Alaska. I remember how sometimes when I flew too close to the mountains, the majestic Alaskan mountain range would loom so large in front of me everything else, like the sky, trees, and rivers, were obscured. However, when I turned toward the east, the mountain took up only some of my visual space. I could look for miles, follow rivers and valleys, and watch the moose wandering around. I loved seeing water wheels, birds, and fishermen in their boats. Once, I saw a bear chasing a moose calf, so I flew directly over them, startled the bear, and that day a calf was saved.

In much the same way, for the past fifty years, trauma has locked out my ability to be present with myself and my ability to be present with others. I was so close to the trauma that all I could see was the pain. I had to step away from the trauma in my life to see the bigger picture. By allowing someone to journey with me, my aperture opened, and I could now see parts of my life that I didn't know existed - spaces between the traumatic events.

One of the ultimate benefits of my journey toward recovery has been the ability to recapture a few good memories from my youth. Perhaps there were days, weeks, or even months in my childhood when I must have enjoyed life without pain. Before counseling, I would never have said that; I only saw the mountain of trauma, Mt. Denali. There was no sky or ground, only rock, ice, or snow and no possibility of life. I felt like I could hardly breathe because I was stuck on the side of a mountain with nothing but icy winds and continual storms.

The following stories are not listed in order of how the people or events impacted my life but when they were released back to my memory. I believe my mind still holds many good memories captive and I look forward to the day when they may be released.

A Coach

I loved sports, but my stepfather said it was a waste of time. He refused to take me to track meets, football games, or tournaments. Thankfully, my mom said it was OK to go if I could find my way there.

Coach Conley was the junior high football, basketball, and track coach. He was a very kind man, appropriately strict, yet somehow able to keep all of us young teenage boys in line. I don't know why he took it upon himself to help me. In retrospect, I believe was it was his firm belief in God and hoping against hope to give me something he saw so clearly was missing. Still, I fondly remember Coach Conley and his little yellow Volkswagen. Without fail, before any event, he went out of his way to park at the end of the road I lived on and pick me up. This meant a great deal to me then and to this day.

One day, there was a minor rebellion at football practice. I don't recall why, but the players disobeyed the coach's instructions and did all the plays in slow motion, with no power, drive, or energy. So, primarily because I appreciated and admired Coach Conley, I refused to go along with the team and flattened the guy I came up against. That started a bit of a kerfuffle right there on the practice field. After we settled down,

I told everyone I was playing for Coach Conley and that they should stop wasting time and do whatever it took to win. That practice quickly turned around, most likely because they knew they'd better be prepared to defend themselves whenever I was involved in a play!

Another vivid memory is etched in my mind. One day Coach picked me up just like he often did. We then embarked on a long drive, heading north of Atlanta, for what was either a state or a tri-county meet; the exact details escape me now, but it was undoubtedly the largest track and field event I'd ever attended. The place was buzzing with people, and every race seemed to fill the stands.

I had quite the workload ahead of me: the 220-meter run, mile run, long jump, and not one but two relays: the 880m and the mile. You see, in track and field, athletes are allowed to compete in four events and two relays, totaling six events. Yet when we arrived, Coach asked me a question. He asked if I'd be interested in trying the triple jump event. I hesitated, admitting I'd never attempted it before. His response was simple. "Well, you're our long jumper, so go for it."

Positioning myself parallel to the other participants, I watched as they performed in the triple jump competition. All too soon it was my turn. I sprinted forward, but my first attempt ended in a scratch. Panic started to set in, but I gave it another shot, only to scratch again. That's when I told myself to slow down and to take it easy. I ran, found my mark, executed the hop, skip, and jump sequence, and suddenly, I found myself atop the leaderboard. The exhilaration was infectious, and everyone around me was ecstatic. Although one competitor managed to edge me out for first place, I proudly took second in an event I'd never even considered before, all because Coach Conley believed in me!

Coach Conley played a pivotal role in my life as he consistently endeavored to be by my side, always available and engaged. That day, I participated in six events, and I medaled in all of them. But the triple jump held a special place in my heart as it brought me immense joy to see Coach brimming with pride in my accomplishments.

I believe when I dropped out of school, Coach Conley felt disappointed that he couldn't continue guiding me. A few months later, I saw him at an automotive store, but I don't think he noticed me. I hid and didn't attempt to approach him: to this day I regret not taking that chance.

Regrettably, I never had another opportunity to express my thanks and share how much he meant to me. Over the years, I've attempted multiple times to locate him so that I could convey to him my gratitude, but my efforts were in vain. Tragically, I learned of his passing and take solace in the belief that I will see him one day in heaven.

A Teacher

Did I tell you that I failed second grade? Who does that? Well, a kid who can't read, that's who. My home life was so catastrophic that we constantly moved. I never started a school year where I finished at the same school until I dropped out of the ninth grade.

As I never maintained good hygiene habits and wet the bed until I was thirteen, I'm sure my smell would have turned most teachers off. Some people are only friendly to others based on their actions or dress. However, Mrs. Rydell, my third-grade teacher, was not that type of person.

I entered the third grade, still trying to read *Fun with Dick and Jane*.[26] However, for some reason, Mrs. Rydell took an interest in me. She was beginning to speak to me using words I had never heard before, words like "You can do it, Johnny," "Try again," and "You're brilliant."

Still, most importantly, she smiled at me, and I remember calling her "Mommy" so many times it must have been embarrassing. With her help and encouragement, by Christmas, I moved from the lowest reading group to the highest one and soon became one of the best readers in the class!

Usually, the love of reading comes from parents who encourage such learning, outstanding early childhood education, and excellent schools. For me, nothing could be further from the truth. I still do not remember my mother ever helping me with my homework.

Mrs. Rydell gave me hope that there was a future for me. Thanks to her, I learned to love reading, or more precisely, that's how my love of words was born. Reading awakened in me a solid and vivid imagination. Books replaced the dirty clothes hamper; no matter where I was, I could be transported to Greece, Rome, or the old Wild West. I now had a safe place of refuge in my mind. Mrs. Rydell is someone I never want to forget.

A Church Lady

Walking to and from one of the many elementary schools I attended, I would often walk by a little church. There I frequently saw an older woman cheerfully standing outside, greeting everyone who passed by, and her smile drew me in for a conversation. She was very kind and challenged me to memorize Psalm 100.[27] If I did, she promised to give me my own Bible.

I didn't know what a Bible was and had no notion of what church or religious life looked like, but I was all about getting something for free. So, I memorized those verses and got my first Bible! Unfortunately, that little Bible was probably left behind on one of our many frantic moves. Though I can't recall her name, I believe the impact of that lady's kindness was one of the points God used to bring me to Himself. [28]

It doesn't matter how little the tyke is or how useless you might think your efforts are; the truth is when you take the time to interact with children, you may have a far more profound impact on their lives than you could ever imagine.

A Surrogate Grandma

The land we were living on in Georgia is now covered with houses, but at that time, it was just fields and pastures as far as the eye could see. A very elderly African American woman, born in the late 1890s, lived in the middle of that land; her name was Daisy. The memories I have of her will forever bring warmth to my heart. Daisy loved having us boys come for a visit. In some ways, she was like a grandmother to us. Somehow, she always had some iced tea and cookies ready to share.

I remember learning many life lessons from her, like how fresh cow milk was so delicious, but if you let it set for any amount of time, you'd better shake it up before taking another drink! She taught us how hospitality and love should carry the day and how important it was always to be kind to everyone we encountered. Daisy was no doubt an oasis for me in an otherwise withering childhood.

Oh, by the way, her churned butter has never been equaled to this day!

A SNOW FALL

Early in my childhood, we lived in Dallas, Texas, before Eddie or any other man came into my life. From our downtown apartment window, I remember being able to see the massive red statue of Pegasus standing on top of the twenty-nine-story Magnolia building. Something was comforting about that winged horse. At night, its neon lights would light up the sky and cast a hue over the windows in the numerous buildings it towered above. Another memory was the big town clock and, using my childhood perspective on the computer, I moved away from both buildings to determine where we might have been living. I must give a shoutout to Google Maps because, from a fragmented childhood memory, after just a few minutes of research on the internet I was able to locate where our apartment might have been!

It was in that apartment that one night, it must have been very late, my mom gently woke me up. "Come and see, Johnny."

Blurry-eyed, I followed her and watched as she opened the front door; it was snowing! That's the first time I remember seeing snow. I marveled at how slowly the snow drifted down; it was so quiet and beautiful as it fell. Mom encouraged us boys to let the flakes fall on our tongues. Aristotle once wrote, "To appreciate the beauty of a snowflake, you must stand out in the cold." He was right. That moment was authentic, without mixture: cold, fun, true, and approached pure joy.

That is a memory of my childhood when I could genuinely say, "All is well." There was no "but" to change it. Mom went into the kitchen, made us all hot chocolate, and we sat, drinking, and watching the quiet snow fall. The value for me today is not so much the joy and peace I remember feeling at that moment; it's the knowledge that such moments are still possible to recollect.

Chapter 8

FINDING MY REAL FATHER

For he who finds Me finds life
and obtains favor from the Lord.
—Proverbs 8:35 (ESV)

IT HAS BEEN INDICATED THAT CHILDREN WHO do not have a relationship with their biological fathers, even though at times there is a social father present, experience adverse psychological consequences.[29] It is often a source of stress and identity confusion. DNA testing is the only way a biological father can be accurately determined in many cases. I knew my biological father's name but never considered him my father. In 1976, when I was twenty-two, I went out of my way to meet him for a moment; I never saw him again. Perhaps DNA is how you found your biological father, but it's not how I found my real father.

LEAVING HOME

Other men came and went, but their temperaments and abuse remained unchanged. I remember leaving home when I was fifteen because the violence had become too much for me. I dropped out at the end of my junior high school year and never stepped foot in high school as a student. Less than two months after my sixteenth birthday, I moved in with my girlfriend's family and married her. A year later, she gave birth to a beautiful little girl, Shawntell. Shortly after that, my young wife left me for an older man. I don't blame her; I was a wreck.

ENLISTING IN THE ARMY

At first, I tried to join the US Air Force but was turned down immediately because I didn't have a high school diploma. Fortunately, after Christmas, I joined the US Army on the 11th of January 1972. After basic training in South Carolina, I miraculously qualified for the Defense Language Institute (DLI) where I was assigned to learn Russian.

The Russian school was no problem. My drinking, however, was! After about six months, the school decided to let me go. So, in the middle of December 1972, I hopped on my motorcycle and headed to Oklahoma for Artillery Advanced Individual Training (AIT).

My drinking problem escorted me all the way. However, as a radio telephone operator (RTO) on a forward observer team, something about the army's business end appealed to me. The discipline, the structure, the relative lack of availability of alcohol, and just plain old time in tents kept me from messing up too badly.

When I finished my training, even though I had volunteered to go to Vietnam, I was sent to Ft. Wainwright, Alaska. There, I went to airborne school and, after some lessons from an Arctic Ranger instructor, became a mountaineering instructor. This allowed me to spend weeks living on glaciers, cross-country skiing, and far away from alcohol.

John on glacier

ACCEPTING A FRIEND

Having just been given my private room, I was furious when they assigned me a roommate. Though raised in an entirely different home environment, Myron accepted me unconditionally. He loved exploring the Alaskan wilderness and even had a blue Chevy truck replete with a snowplow to handle any off-road travels. We went out exploring on the weekends and had a blast. However, the condition for joining him on Sundays was that I had to go with him to church first. That's when I was first introduced to church, spirituality, and faith. "I'm not coming back just to get you," he'd say. "If you want to go with me, you must come now."

Growing up, I did not believe in God; I had no reason to. However, I remember being impressed by a photo published on Christmas Eve in 1968 entitled "Earthrise." A photograph of a beautiful blue marble against the dark vastness of space was taken from the moon's surface. That photo caused me to contemplate

Earthrise

the fundamental impossibility of our existence in this incomprehensibly large universe we call home.

BECOMING A CHILD OF GOD

I soon began reading a book I had never read, the Bible. Actually, at first it was an illustrated children's book at a doctor's office with Bible stories in it. Yet in time, I read more and more of the Bible. Through reading it, I came to believe in the truth that there is a God, a heaven, and a hell. I understood there was only one path to heaven, and I wasn't on it! I asked God to forgive me and wholeheartedly adopted the Christian life and values. I had found my real father; I was a child of God!

In large part, this poor ragamuffin from Texas, this feral child who dropped out of school in junior high, owes all his accomplishments to a teacher who took the time to teach him how to read and a fellow soldier who, through his unconditional friendship, introduced him to his real father, God!

BECOMING A CHAPLAIN

In 1974, I volunteered as a counselor at a Bible camp in central Alaska. There I fell in love with Barbara. That fall I was transferred to Arizona, and we had to "date" by weekly pay phone calls and mail. In 1975, I decided to reenlist, become a warrant officer, and fly helicopters. So, in December, I took a hop to Alaska and asked Barbara to marry me. Life was good!

God soon changed my plan however, and I felt Him leading me to become a chaplain. That's what I wanted to be: someone others could turn to in times of trouble, someone to help them find hope. As I researched the requirements to become a chaplain, I quickly learned it was out of the question. I would have to graduate from high school, earn a bachelor's degree and a master's degree, and then have two years of practical experience!

So, I took an honorable discharge from the army, Barbara and I married in August, and I began the next phase of my life's journey. Twenty years later, though, after completing all the requirements necessary, I was able to start another career as a United States Air Force chaplain!

Chapter 9

THROUGH THE EYES OF A CHILD

Don't judge a book by its cover.[30]
—George Eliot

JEANNE SHINSKEY, BABY LAB DIRECTOR IN THE Department of Psychology at the Royal Holloway University of London, wrote, "It's important to remember that, even if we can't explicitly remember specific events from when we were very young, their accumulation nevertheless leaves lasting traces that influence our behavior. The first few years of life are paradoxically forgettable and powerful in shaping the adults we become."[31]

On my journey toward recovery, my counselor often asked me where my strength came from. "Without someone 'parenting' you," he would say, "you would most likely not have compassion if compassion had not been shown to you in your early childhood."

He said that having been raised the way I was, there must have been something or someone in my life that had helped shape me. I agreed, for otherwise, I would be in prison, a drug addict, or dead for many reasons. However, try as I might, no person came to me; there was only emptiness. I would look at him blankly and answer, "I don't know."

Importance of Parents

It was 2:55 a.m. when I abruptly woke up. Since sleep was evading me, I got out of bed and, by 3:35 a.m., was sitting in front of the computer pondering my counselor's words. That's when I remembered someone in my life who had parented me!

Parents comprise a mother and father. That's the way it is, that's reality, right? However, any number of questions come to mind. What about a child raised in an orphanage? Who takes care of them? Who changes, cuddles, and feeds them? Who educates them? What about the parenting of children who share my early childhood circumstances? What about the child raised by their grandparents, aunt, sister, brother, or the friendly couple down the street? Do they have parents? My mother and father divorced when I was just over a year old. Who were my parents?

One may vigorously argue what parenting should be, but to say that the only way to be a parent is to be one biologically is absurd. One may be a biological parent and be not much more than a sperm or egg donor. In a human relationship, being a parent requires leading, guiding, and nurturing aspects.

I remember reading that during World War II in England, children without parenting, deprived of touch, would become morose—analytically depressed—and often die. Anaclitic is a fancy word that means to support oneself. In the case of these children, when there was no one to support them, despite adequate nutrition and proper hygiene, they often died.

Logically then, in my case, one may be inclined to agree that some form of parenting must have been provided. Otherwise, I would not have survived or would have suffered significant emotional and physical harm.

MY UNCLE DAVID

This morning, however, was different. Why? Well, in some ways, I've known this all along. One of the extraordinary things about recovering memories is that as soon as they are remembered, you realize they were always there, just inaccessible.

Why now? Perhaps it was because while writing this book, my mind had been focused on my childhood memories, but no, I knew it was much more than that. The previous night, Barbara and I had watched an episode of the British show *Grantchester*. Set in the 1950s, one of the characters, Leonard, a member of the clergy engaged as an assistant to a parish priest, had been accused of "gross indecency," a criminal charge of homosexual conduct. While Leonard's friends unfalteringly supported him, he was nevertheless put on trial.

At the courthouse, Leonard immediately pled guilty. He was exhausted from living a lie. The mean-spirited prosecutor then mercilessly berated him, saying, "God can't possibly love you."

Leonard, broken, sobbed, "I've always doubted that He could love me."

Will, the parish priest, was furious and, despite everyone's warnings, spoke publicly at the trial on Leonard's behalf. Will told the judge, "Leonard wasn't worried for himself today but for me. I consider him a brother. Please don't punish him further."

While watching that show, the impact I felt was great sadness. Indeed, it is only now that I realized that I'm "Will", and "Leonard" is my uncle David.

David was a lifelong and proud member of the gay community. He loved to wear clothing that was expressive of his sexual identity as a gay man; he was cheerful, thoughtful, and sensitive. He had a Southern charm and a laugh that was contagious. That David, and his partner Jerry, chose to attend my graduation from seminary in 1987 remains to me a sign of his love.

Years ago, for a class assignment at Boston University, I interviewed Uncle David for a study I was conducting on the aging gay population. When I asked if he would answer some very personal questions, David said, "Johnny, ask me anything you want, and I'll tell you what you want to know."

David said that he moved in with my mother in 1957 because my grandfather told him that he cared "no more for your [David's] feelings than that dog lying there."

Apparently, he lived with us off and on for five years, from 1957 until 1962. He shared how he often bathed, clothed, and tucked us boys into bed or got us ready for school the next morning. Reflecting on this, I realize now that my only stable male figure was my uncle David.

The final words of our phone call were not expected. "Johnny, I love you, son."

Outside the typical common usage in the South, no man had ever called me "son". The men in my life called me boy, kid, or more often, stupid. His words were as natural as the morning dew, as was my response. "I love you, too."

How was I parented for all those years that I cannot remember? Still, even though I don't remember much, I know something more deeply. My experience with Uncle David was far more significant than my memories of him. Those memories were put into the vault of my heart, only now to be reflected on with any sense of complete understanding and appreciation.

Yes, I grew up in challenging surroundings, yet all my memories of rescue and care from a male, other than Coach Conley, were from David. When I was seven or eight, I nearly drowned in the Gulf of Mexico when a vicious undertow caught me and churned my body in circles under the waves. My breath was almost gone and, tumbling repeatedly, I could not stand up. It was David who dove into the water and rescued me. Without him, I would most assuredly have drowned.

During the summer in the sixties, many of the streets in the South were covered with tar. The heat would melt the tar, and since we boys were always barefoot no matter where we went, we made a game out of running on the road as long as we could. The object was to see who could stay on the hot pavement the longest. By the time we were done, we had tar covering the bottom of our feet so one by one, we'd turn off into the grass to cool down and peel the hardened tar off our feet. So much fun! (Please don't try this yourself!

Once, when we were at Grandma's house, I ran around barefoot as usual. The only difference this time was that we were on a farm in the middle of wild Texas, not in the nice Houston grass. As I ran into the backyard, it took a moment to realize the pain; I couldn't move because my feet were covered with little Texas burrs. I immediately cried out for help. David quickly came out, picked me up, and carried me to the porch as I wailed. Then I remember how he carefully pulled each burr from the

bottom of my feet. He was there for me just like when he rescued me from a dreadful undertow in the Gulf of Mexico.

THE SOURCE OF WHO I AM

On my journey toward recovery, I discovered that much of my stability as an adult was derived from my early childhood. I had a mother who loved me as best as she could and an uncle who cared for me. Through the eyes of a very young child, it seemed perfectly natural. A child sees no agreement or disagreement politically, theologically, culturally, or socially. Instead, the child sees and comprehends love or nonlove as well as care or non-care.

David told me that he had not faced any real discrimination. He said, "Life has been good."

Yet in the same breath, he told me how, after Grandma died, the church she was a member of for over forty years sent a delegation to see if David would like to help at the funeral. One look at David and Jerry, and they never came back. That committee neither honored my grandmother's memory nor God's commandments.

I visited and chatted with David a few years ago, just before he died. He was somber as I tried to pry from him some information about my past. He didn't want to go there, but he shared with me an event I had never known. David said that one day he was fighting with Eddie. It quickly turned into a scene one might see depicted in a TV crime drama, but this was real. For whatever reason, Eddie pulled out his pistol, a .38 Special, cocked it, put it to David's head, and with expletive language, proceeded to scream out that he was going to blow David's brains out. Mom, tears streaming down her face, begged Eddie not to kill David.

I was shocked. Why couldn't I remember any of it? I didn't know what to say. David looked greatly disappointed. With his profoundly Southern accent, he sadly said, "Johnny, you were there! You saw it all!"

Looking back now, I guess his deep disappointment was finding out that the only living witness to his trauma, me, had no memory of it. Perhaps that traumatic event was the one that lowered the curtain over my childhood memories. I am still absorbing the fact that, outside my real Father, God, the source of my compassion, kindness, and even the tenderness that flows through me, was likely gained from a small window of life I had with my Uncle David.

Chapter 10

WHO AM I?

I wasn't searching for something or someone
...I was searching for me.[32]
-Carrie Bradshaw

PERHAPS YOU HAVE READ THE FAMOUS ANCIENT
Greek saying, "Know thyself." However, do you know why knowing
yourself is important? Knowing yourself helps you develop sympathy
and expands your awareness of the feelings and emotions of other people.
After a traumatic experience, you'll suddenly realize you no longer know
who you are.

Here's what happened: That event in your life took so much of your
time and energy that you had to put yourself on hold to survive. Do you
even remember what you were like or what you enjoyed? This chapter
"Who Am I?" is all about how my journey toward recovery has helped
me find answers to that question.

Who Was I Then?

As I have previously mentioned, my life has been circumscribed by war.
Those wars caused both direct and indirect trauma. The problem is that the
trauma you experienced is carried inside you. It is always there with you:
beside you, in front of you, behind you, enveloping you. Nothing can change
a traumatic event. The experience was real; it's what happened. Posttraumatic
stress disorder (PTSD) is a mental health condition triggered by a traumatic
event—experiencing or witnessing it. It can produce a profound sense of
aloneness, which only the counseling process can help reduce.

In this "anthology," I used the metaphor of Medusa to show, in graphic form, the damage that trauma brings into a person's life. It turns people into stone as they try to dissociate from the pain. You may be able to forget the traumatic events, but they will always remain in your body; remember how Dr. Bezel Van der Kolk said, "The body keeps the score"?[33]

When I accepted Christ as my Savior, I was saved and gained a relationship with God. Though God has promised us that we will be fully healed in heaven, while on this earth, we can never be cured of every pain or sorrow. Thankfully, with the power of God, through the Holy Spirit, we can still learn how to carry on and carry on well. Even though I have not seen the Holy Spirit visually, I have sensed His presence, goodness, and power.

However, God also created us with the fundamental need for others; we need someone to journey with, to see, hear, touch, and talk with. We must not push others away; we must not turn them into stone.

Who Am I Now?

As a chaplain in the military, I was given many unique opportunities. One was that I was able to learn several personality instruments. I'm trained in seven different instruments and certified to teach the trainer in one of them. All these personality instruments evaluate individuals based on the enduring qualities they possess. Most are based on the four significant personality distinctions: sanguine, choleric, melancholic, and phlegmatic.

Out of all these personality instruments, Don Lowery's True Colors is particularly informative.[34] Created in 1978 for his children, Dr. Lowery observed that colors are often used to describe others, such as true blue, pure gold, green with envy, or red with anger. So, by taking the four primary personality categories, he assigned colors to them. This concept became wildly successful because it was simple to understand and available for all ages.

My top two colors are blue and green. To understand what that means, you must first understand what those colors indicate. Blues are deeply idealistic, spiritual, sincere, and peaceful, and they are usually imaginative, flexible, sympathetic, empathetic, warm, communicative, compassionate, and personal.

However, separated by only a point, green was my next dominant color. Now green indicates an inventive, logical person and a problem-solver. They enjoy challenges and are very independent thinkers and investigators; for them, work is play.

When embodied in the same person, these two colors do not lie easily next to each other. Sometimes, when empathy was called for in a blue situation, I would act entirely green, looking more for competence. Or in some cases when competence was called for, I would look more for empathy. Consequently, the way I have responded has not always been consistent.

About twenty years ago, noticing my internal struggles, my wife created a small helping device for me to carry in my pocket: a BLUE and GREEN bead tied together by a tiny string. That way, when I talked to a base commander, I could touch the GREEN bead, and it would remind me to stay in my GREEN mode because the commander was looking for competence, fixing problems, and making things operate as they should. However, I would touch the BLUE bead when I had someone in my office for counseling. They didn't need discipline or a lecture about time management; they needed empathy, someone to come alongside them and encourage them.

I have carried a touchstone like those beads in my pocket for years; sometimes beads, sometimes rocks, even once they were colored shells. Occasionally, I would set them in front of my computer screen because it's very beneficial to be reminded of the importance of using my colors in the right situation.

Looking back, I realize those two colors have always conflicted. I now understand why, as an eight-year-old, when the nurse accidentally ran over my pet puppy, Bourbon, I couldn't let her comfort me; I was already broken. My GREEN easily obstructed me from showing my emotional pain before her. My BLUE would have allowed her to be there with me; we could have comforted one another. I felt her pain, but I couldn't help her because my GREEN had become the primary part of who I was.

Since then, part of my journey toward recovery has been to regain the BLUE that had been dormant for years. GREEN was my protector, my shield in many ways, and I am deeply indebted for that. GREEN will always be a part of me, but the more I become present with others, the more I realize that I must learn to live with both colors simultaneously. I am not complete without either one of them.

WHO CAN I BE?

As I mentioned in chapter 3, the winged horse Pegasus was born when Perseus beheaded Medusa and released her from her trauma. As a boy, I never knew that Medusa and Pegasus were related. That his birth was brought about entirely by her death was outside of my awareness. Yet the wonder of Pegasus and his ability to fly only came only after Medusa's trauma ended. One of my favorite biblical passages is Isaiah 61:1–3 (ESV):

> The Spirit of the Lord God is upon me,
>   because the Lord has anointed me
>   to bring good news to the poor;
> He has sent me to bind up the brokenhearted,
>   to proclaim liberty to the captives,
>   and the opening of the prison to those who are bound;
> to proclaim the year of the Lord's favor,
>   and the day of vengeance of our God;
>   to comfort all who mourn;
> to grant to those who mourn in Zion—
>   to give them a beautiful headdress instead of ashes,
>   the oil of gladness instead of mourning,
>   the garment of praise instead of a faint spirit;
>   that they may be called oaks of righteousness,
>   the planting of the Lord that he may be glorified.

Even though this passage interpretively has to do with the people of Israel in general and Jerusalem in particular, it also reveals something to us about the heart of God. He delights in transforming wounded, grief-stricken, and bound captives into freedom-loving, praise-extolling pillars of righteous people.

God has the heart of a true poet; He can transform our ashes and traumas into beauty. Isaiah 61:1–3 implies that the ashes are directly tied to grief, pain, loss, and hopelessness. Ashes are created from what trauma has destroyed: our dreams, family, hopes, desires, and goals. They are formed as the fuel of our lives is burned up and we try to keep the creeping cold away from our souls.

When trauma comes, and Medusa is looking straight at you, and you feel yourself turning to stone, join me in saying, "I'm still alive! With God's power, there is a healing for me yet!" He promises to make something beautiful from our ashes.

Chapter 11

GOD'S DESIGN

The one and only God, the Creator of
the universe, the great "I am,"
knows our frames, and by the Word of His power
promises to uphold our very being.
Hebrews 1:3 (ESV)

TRAUMA AND PAIN ARE TWO OF THE MOST difficult things that anyone has to deal with in life. Whether it's experiencing a personal tragedy or witnessing someone else's suffering, the impact can be profound and long-lasting. But did you know that God has personally demonstrated how we can help ourselves and others who have experienced trauma and pain? It's true! In fact, one of the least utilized yet most instructive passages in the Bible on this topic can be found in 1 Kings 18-19.

In this passage, we see Elijah, one of God's prophets, facing deep trauma and pain. He had just experienced a major victory over the prophets of Baal, but he was still being pursued by Queen Jezebel, who threatened to kill him. Elijah was so overwhelmed that he fled into the wilderness and begged God to take his life. But instead of abandoning him, God sent an angel to provide food and water and then spoke to him in a still, small voice.

God's response to Elijah is very instructive about how we, too, can help ourselves and others heal. First, God acknowledged Elijah's pain and didn't minimize it. Second, He provided practical help and support in the form of food and water. And finally, He spoke to Elijah in a gentle, calming voice, reminding him of his purpose and giving him hope for the future.

We can apply these same principles when helping ourselves or others who are dealing with trauma and pain. By acknowledging the pain, providing practical help and support, and offering words of encouragement and hope, we can help ourselves and others heal and move forward in life.

Elijah was a fierce and determined prophet, who emerged on the scene with a sense of bravado and confidence that was matched by few others. He was a man of great faith, who had challenged King Ahab, Queen Jezebel, and the prophets of Baal and Asherah to a trial by fire, which culminated in the death of over 850 people. Despite the immense pressure and opposition he faced, Elijah remained steadfast in his convictions, and continued to speak truth to power, even when it was unpopular to do so. His unwavering commitment to his beliefs, and his willingness to stand up for what was right, made him a hero to many, and a symbol of hope in troubled times. Though his story is one of great tragedy and triumph, Elijah's legacy lives on, inspiring generations to come to stand up for what they believe in, no matter the cost.

As a firsthand witness to the suffering caused by war, I am convinced that the vast majority of commentators[35] who have written about this passage, did not utilize the lens of a trauma survivor. They viewed Elijah's response, running away and hiding in a cave, as "faithlessness" and a "failure." Elijah's experience on Mt Carmel, devastated his image of God, not because he lacked faith or loyalty, but because his initial image of God collided with the reality he experienced.

As a counselor, though there is no way of knowing Elijah's thoughts, I would have no trouble diagnosing Elijah with Acute Stress Disorder (ASD), and at a minimum, he exhibited Post-Traumatic Stress (PTS) symptoms. It's clear that Elijah had been through a lot, and his experiences had taken a significant toll on his mental well-being.

While reading Elijah's story, I can hear his possible unspoken questions to God, such as, "Haven't I given all to you? Haven't I risked my life? Don't I deserve better than this?" It's understandable that after all he had been through, Elijah is questioning why he has had to endure such hardship and suffering.

As a counselor, it's my responsibility to help Elijah work through these feelings and emotions. We'll work to identify coping mechanisms that can help him manage his symptoms, and we'll explore the root causes of his stress and anxiety. Together, we'll work towards a path of healing and recovery, so that Elijah can move forward with hope and resilience.

The parallels between Elijah and current trauma survivors are strikingly similar. Is it any surprise that Elijah, a mighty prophet of God, when faced with the threat of death by Queen Jezebel, suddenly and seemingly inexplicably became fearful, discouraged, and ran for his life? I contend that Elijah's spiritual, physical, and emotional issues were not a result of a loss of courage or faith but a result of trauma. As all the people killed were his fellow countrymen, could it be that he was suffering from a moral injury?

When reading this passage, it is easy to see how Elijah's thoughts caused him profound depression and suicidal ideations. Howell and Howell note that Elijah's response to Israel's failure to renew their relationship with God was one of hopelessness.[36] It was this hopelessness that brought about his negative view of self, his future, and his experience.

Elijah was traumatized in body, mind, and spirit, and God, like He does for us, tenderly saw to his well-being. God did not punish, chastise, or even get upset with Elijah. This was not a failure on Elijah's part. God wrote Maslow's hierarchy of needs[37] on the hearts of men and women millennia before Maslow put it on paper.

In 2010-11, I was the senior chaplain advisor at the USAF Deployment Transition Center (DTC) located in Germany at Ramstein Air Base. There, our team designed a four-day program to assist personnel who had been exposed to Combat Stress in transitioning back to their home station. This ConOps (Concept of Operations) program listed six objectives: Rest, Recapture, Recreate, Reintegrate, Reflect, and Resource. It shouldn't be too amazing to comprehend that these are the same six steps that God walked Elijah through!

REST

God created us; the Lord knows that our bodies need care (Psalm 103:14). God has ordained sleep and rest as necessary for our survival and ability to function, so the Lord allowed Elijah time to sleep. Rest not only refreshes the body but also the spirit.

Often, physicians tell patients, "Get plenty of rest." However, the patient is never told what rest is. The American Heritage Medical Dictionary states that rest can be divided into three general areas: freedom from physical activity, freedom from responsibility, and, of course, physical sleep.[38] According to the Veterans Administration and the Department of Defense (VA/DOD), the inability to rest is one of the most common symptoms following a traumatic event.[39] During a pastoral counseling course at Dallas Theological Seminary, presented by well-known psychiatrists Dr. Frank Minrith and Dr. Paul Meier, Dr. Minrith stated, "Once a person is admitted to the hospital psychiatric ward, if we let them sleep for one or two days fully half of their presenting symptoms simply disappeared".[40]

Rest can take on many forms depending on the individuals want needs and desires. Here are some possibilities:

- **Physical Rest**: This involves allowing your body to recover and rejuvenate through activities like sleeping, napping, or low-intensity exercises such as walking or gentle stretching.
- **Mental Rest**: Mental rest involves taking a break from stimulation and stress. This may involve activities such as meditation, mindfulness practices, or simply taking quiet time to relax and unwind without distractions.
- **Emotional Rest**: Emotional rest involves acknowledging and addressing your feelings, whether through journaling, talking with a trusted friend or therapist, or engaging in activities that bring you joy and comfort.
- **Social Rest**: Social rest involves setting boundaries and taking time away from social interactions when needed. This could mean saying no to social invitations, taking a break from social

media, or spending time alone or with a small, supportive group of loved ones.

- **Creative Rest**: Creative rest involves stepping away from your usual endeavors to allow your mind to recharge and find inspiration. This might involve engaging in different activities, exploring new hobbies, or simply giving yourself permission to relax without feeling the pressure to be productive.
- **Spiritual Rest**: Spiritual rest involves nourishing your soul and connecting with something greater than yourself. This could include practices such as prayer, meditation, spending time in nature, or engaging in activities that bring you a sense of purpose and fulfillment.

Rest is all about respecting and taking care of your physical, mental, and spiritual health. It involves giving yourself the necessary time and environment to recharge and restore your energy levels. It is vital to pay attention to your individual needs and discover what methods of relaxation and rest work best for you.

RECAPTURE

God began a recapture or reintegration, plan for Elijah in 1 Kings 19:5 when He sent "*the* angel of the LORD" to him as opposed to, in verse 7, "*an* angel of the LORD." "The angel of the LORD", in Protestant Evangelicalism, is considered a Theophany, that is, a description used in the Old Testament of a special manifestation of God, or more accurately, a Christophany--a manifestation of Christ.[41] The Catholic Church takes "the angel of the Lord" as an angel bearing the name of God.[42] Regardless of how you interpret it, the angel of the LORD demonstrated to Elijah that he was still the object of God's love and showed him relationship, care, and community.

The angel also touched Elijah and provided him with some things fundamental for survival, such as food and water. Twice, Elijah is told to eat and drink, and twice, he is allowed to sleep. God knew that one brief encounter would not sustain Elijah in his current state. In the same way, there cannot be a one-size-fits-all program for trauma survivors. They must be allowed to rest and eat; each person will be on their own timetable.

God also provided Elijah with an environment, a safe space, where he could begin healing. If you have ever had to survive in the wilderness, you understand how building a fire significantly increases your ability to survive both physically and mentally.[43] The fire provides warmth, light, food, protection, and a sense of control. Trauma survivors need touch, food, and warmth as well – they need this so that they can press on towards physical and psychological health.

In verse ten, Elijah's response seems to blame God and does not seem to appreciate of the provisions sent to him. Was he taking God for granted? No, God knew that the capacity for response and appreciation comes only after time. To negatively judge Elijah's response belies a lack of comprehension of Post-Traumatic Stress (PTS).

It's important to keep in mind that it's not uncommon for trauma survivors to have an apparent lack of appreciation. If you're expecting them to give you a big hug and a thank you, you may be greatly disappointed. However, please don't be discouraged by this. Just like how Elijah did not appreciate God's provision, many trauma survivors may not appreciate your help. But that doesn't mean that your efforts are in vain. They might, however, as Elijah did, avail themselves of the provisions offered, and that will bring them comfort. So, it's crucial to continue offering your support and care with patience and understanding, even if the response from the person you're helping isn't what you expected. Remember, your assistance can make a huge difference in their healing process, so keep up the good work!

RECREATE

The journey towards healing and recovery can be a long and grueling one, particularly for those who have experienced traumatic events. Trauma can leave deep and lasting scars on both the mind and body, making it difficult to move forward and find peace. However, physical activity can play a crucial role in helping survivors rebuild their lives and regain a sense of control and empowerment. By engaging in exercise and other forms of physical activity, survivors can improve their physical health, boost their mood, and reduce symptoms of anxiety and depression.

It is essential to recognize the importance of exercise in the process of recovery. After all, the benefits of physical activity are well-documented. Exercise can help to reduce stress, improve sleep quality, and increase self-esteem and confidence. Moreover, by engaging in physical activity, survivors can develop a sense of mastery over their bodies and their lives, which can be incredibly empowering.

Interestingly, the Bible provides an example of the healing power of physical activity. In 1 Kings 19:7-8, we learn that after experiencing trauma, Elijah arose and ate and drank, and went to Horeb, the mountain of God. It is not entirely clear why Elijah chose to go to the mountain of God. Perhaps he was seeking a peaceful place to die, as he had expressed a desire to do so. Or maybe he was in search of God, as he ultimately did find Him. Whatever the reason, what is clear is that Elijah took action and went to the mountain.

In many ways, this story highlights the importance of taking action in the face of trauma. While it can be tempting to withdraw and retreat from the world after experiencing a traumatic event, it is often more helpful to take positive steps towards healing and recovery. By engaging in physical activity and other forms of self-care, survivors can begin to rebuild their lives and find hope and healing in the midst of their pain.

Similarly, trauma survivors can take action towards their own healing and recovery by engaging in physical activity. Exercise can help individuals release pent-up emotions, reduce stress, and increase feelings of self-worth and confidence. By engaging in physical activity, survivors can take a step towards reconstructing and recreating their lives.

Overall, the story of Elijah reminds us that healing and recovery are possible, even in the face of trauma. It is up to each individual to take action and seek out the resources and support they need to move forward. With dedication and effort, survivors can find their way to a brighter future.

The text reveals that, "he went in the strength of that food forty days and forty nights to Horeb." The forty days and forty nights are not without significance. From where Elijah began, a day's journey south of Beersheba, he was no forty days and nights from Horeb. A straight trip from the broom tree would have required little more than seven, maybe eight days. It seems clear that he was simply wandering about much like the children of Israel had done for forty years. Elijah spent forty days miraculously sustained by God on the very mountain Moses received the Ten Commandments (Exodus 34:28). What was Elijah thinking about during that time? We are never told.

REINTEGRATE

God told Elijah to come out of the cave and stand before Him - Elijah's reintegration process was about to begin. First, there was a mighty wind that shattered rock around Elijah. Second, an earthquake shook the ground under Elijah's feet. Third, a fire engulfed the area but did not consume him. In all these manifestations, however, God was not there. These were mere precursors to God's appearance.[44]

According to Dr. Judith Herman, the three stages of recovery from trauma are: [45]

1) Establishing safety
2) Reconstructing the traumatic story
3) Restoring the connection between the survivor and their community

Elijah had been on a difficult journey, physically and emotionally. He had fled from Jezebel, who had vowed to kill him because of his prophetic work. He had traveled for forty days and nights through the wilderness with no food or water. But then, something miraculous happened. An angel of the Lord appeared to him and provided food and drink. Elijah's physical and spiritual strength began to grow, and he finally found himself in a place of safety and rest.

Now, because of his improved condition, Elijah was poised to reflect on all that had happened and begin to consciously reintegrate into society. He even had a place of shelter: Many believe that the cave Elijah was in may well be "the cleft of the rock"[46] on Mount Horeb, where God's glory passed by Moses (Exodus 33:21-33). Given that God is a God of irony, this would come as no surprise.

As Elijah rested in the cave, he must have contemplated the events that had led him there. He had been a faithful servant of God, but his work had made him a target of those in power. He had endured great hardship and danger, but through it all, he had remained faithful. Now, in this quiet place, he had the opportunity to reflect on his journey and reorient himself to his purpose.

The cave on Mount Horeb was a fitting place for Elijah to rest and reflect. It was a place where God's glory had been revealed to Moses, and now it was a place where Elijah could experience God's presence and find renewal. As he looked back on his journey and looked forward to the future, Elijah knew that he could trust in God's faithfulness and provision, no matter what lay ahead.

REFLECT

God then began a healing dialogue with Elijah and asked the question, "Why are you here, Elijah?" This question was designed not to chastise as Davies argues, [46] but was an opportunity for Elijah to take the darkness of his thoughts and put them outside of himself. Even if Davies is correct in stating that Elijah's condition contained delusions of self-importance and paranoia,[47] these reactions are normal responses to traumatic stress. God's purpose was not to judge, condemn, or criticize; it was to bring about healing through dialogue. God desires us to communicate our pain to Him as well.

Trauma survivors often find it difficult to come to terms with the events that have caused them immense pain and suffering. They struggle to integrate those events into their life and as a result, they end up repeating themselves. This is where the concept of "the talking cure"[48] comes into play. According to Freud, it is essential to talk about one's traumatic experiences in order to begin the healing process.[49] Traumatic Reenactment is a term that Freud used to describe how survivors repeat past events without even realizing that they are doing so. It is their way of remembering what happened to them.

In the book "Trauma and Recovery," Judith Herman argues that it is only when the truth is fully recognized that survivors can begin their recovery.[50] Unfortunately, secrecy often prevails, and the story of the traumatic event surfaces not as a verbal narrative but as a symptom. This is why it is so important to ask trauma survivors the question "Why are you here?" in the same compassionate spirit as God asked Elijah.

We all have stories to tell, and trauma survivors need to tell theirs in order to begin their healing journey. Only by sharing their experiences can they fully process what has happened to them and start to move forward. It takes time, patience, and empathy to help survivors feel safe enough to open up and share their stories. But with the right support and guidance, they can eventually find their voice and reclaim their sense of self.

RESOURCES

If you are a trauma survivor, you may feel like you're alone, especially if you're not aware of the support system available to you. However, it's essential to know that there are resources out there that could significantly impact your journey towards healing. You can find some of these resources in the appendixes of this book. The purpose of this chapter is to give you hope that you have a future. There is always a possibility of reconnecting with significant others and renewing your relationship with God, who is the one and only Creator of the universe. He is the great "I am" and knows everything about us, even our frames. By the Word of His power, He promises to uphold and sustain us (Hebrews 1:3).

As someone who has been on the journey towards recovery, I can say that the primary objective for trauma survivors is to establish stability in all aspects of their lives - physical, psychological, and spiritual. We can talk to God without fear of retribution, and in doing so, we will eventually be able to pick up our "mantle" and continue moving forward like Elijah did. As you continue on your journey towards recovery you will soon begin to break through Medusa's hold on you! Remember that you're not alone, and there is always hope for a better tomorrow.

Conclusion

He will cover you with his pinions,
and under his wings you will find refuge;
his faithfulness is a shield and buckler.
You will not fear the terror of the night,
nor the arrow that flies by day,
nor the pestilence that stalks in darkness,
nor the destruction that wastes at noonday.
—Psalm 91:4–6 (ESV)

NO ONE SHOULD FACE THEIR CHILDHOOD terrors alone. Since the individuals present with me in my childhood are unable to talk about them, I'm very thankful to have found several people willing to go on this journey toward recovery with me. I needed to remember these things with you so that in remembering them together we might see the hand of God in all of them.

I want to leave you with the six steps I have learned on my journey toward recovery and trust they will help you as well:

1. **Do not minimize or dismiss your trauma.**

   The healing process can be a challenging journey, but it begins with acknowledging the trauma and realizing that you are not to blame. This is an important step towards your recovery and well-being. It's important to remember that accepting or acknowledging something that happened in the past doesn't mean you agree or condone it. It simply means that you are taking ownership of your experiences and starting to move towards healing.

   If you've experienced trauma at the hands of "loved ones," you may have been gaslighted all your life. Gaslighting is a form of psychological manipulation in which the abuser attempts to sow self-doubt and confusion in the victim's mind. Gaslighters seek to gain power and control over the other person by distorting reality and forcing them to question their judgment and intuition. It can be a devastating experience, and it's important to recognize that it is not your fault. Don't gaslight yourself by pretending it didn't happen or blaming yourself.

Remember, healing takes time and effort. It's a journey that may have ups and downs, but with support and self-care, you can overcome the trauma and move forward towards a healthier and happier life. Seek help from trusted friends, family members, or professionals if you need it. You deserve to live a life free from the pain of past trauma.

2. Do not isolate yourself: Get help!

As a trauma survivor, I have always found it difficult to connect with others. Isolation became my safe haven, and I felt most comfortable alone. The safest I've ever felt was when I was spelunking in a small cave in Arizona. It was just me and the darkness, and for a moment, I was free from the pain and fear that had haunted me for so long. No one knew I was there, and even if they did, they could not find me.

But as I've grown older, I've come to realize that connecting with others is healing. It's not easy to open up and share our deepest fears and struggles, but it's necessary if we want to move forward and heal. It can be terrifying to make ourselves vulnerable, but it's worth it.

If you're struggling, I encourage you to make an offer of trust to someone you feel safe with. It could be a family member, a friend, or a counselor. You may be surprised to see how they respond and how willing they are to journey with you. It's never too late to seek help and to start on the path to healing.

3. Take care of your health.

One of the most incredible things I remember hearing about trauma was from Dr. Van der Kolk. He said something along the lines of, "With trauma, sometimes it's more important to do yoga than counseling." [51] At first, this statement might seem a little strange, but when you think about it, it actually makes a lot of sense.

Trauma is not just a mental experience; it also has a strong physical component. When we experience trauma, our bodies undergo significant changes in response to the stress. These changes can include an increase in heart rate, blood pressure, and the release of certain hormones such as adrenaline and cortisol.

These physical changes can have a long-lasting impact on our bodies, making it harder for us to cope with stress in the future. This is where van Der Kolk says yoga comes in. Yoga is a great way to help us manage stress and improve our overall health; in some cases better than counseling. This can be especially helpful for those who have experienced trauma, as it can be difficult to connect with our bodies and emotions after a traumatic event.

So, while counseling is certainly an important part of the healing process for trauma survivors, it's also important to remember the role that physical health and well-being can play. By incorporating exercise into our daily lives, we can improve our ability to cope with stress and move towards a more balanced and healthy life.

4. **Pursue meaning, and healing will follow.**

I had focused on healing for many years, trying different methods and approaches, but it always seemed to elude me with certainty. The healing process can be a difficult and complex journey, and I often felt lost and frustrated along the way. However, I never gave up hope and kept searching for the right path to take.

Fortunately, I found my journeying partners who have played a significant role in my healing journey. They have been my support system, offering guidance, love, and encouragement every step of the way. Together, we have navigated through choppy waters, and although my story may seem disjointed and confusing at times, I have managed to stitch together a narrative that makes sense to me.

The initial purpose of establishing a narrative was to help me make sense of my experiences and find a way to heal from them. Through the process of creating this narrative, I have gained a deeper understanding of myself and my journey. I have uncovered hidden truths and have come to accept certain aspects of my life that I once struggled with. My new narrative is one that is closer to reality and one that is much more satisfying. I am grateful for the journey and for the people who have helped me along the way. I now feel more grounded and at peace with myself, and I am excited to see what the future holds.

5. Be patient with yourself.

It's important to remember to be patient with yourself when working through childhood trauma. It's not an easy or quick process, and there will be times when you may feel like giving up. But don't give up. Keep pushing through, and celebrate the small victories along the way. Each success, no matter how small, is a step towards healing. Before you know it, those small victories can turn into a landslide of childhood trauma healing. Just remember to take it one step at a time, be kind to yourself, and keep moving forward.

6. Believe in a higher power - God.

The Alcoholics Anonymous (AA) program[52] has been a beacon of hope for millions of people struggling with addiction. One of its twelve steps involves believing in a Higher Power that can provide the strength needed to overcome addiction. As an atheist, I initially struggled with this step, but when I started living my life as a child of the one true God, the God of the Bible, I found the strength I needed to begin my journey toward recovery.

Trusting in Jesus Christ as my Savior has been the key to my transformation. It has given me a sense of purpose and direction that I had never experienced before. Through this faith, I have discovered how precious and valuable I truly am, and I have been able to let go of the shame and guilt that had been holding me back.

If you are struggling with addiction, I encourage you to consider this path toward recovery. It may seem daunting at first, but with the help of a supportive community and a belief in God, you can find the strength and courage to overcome your addiction and live a fulfilling life. Remember, you are not alone, and there is hope for a better tomorrow.

This was not an easy book to write; parts may have been challenging to read, and indeed, it was not easy to experience. I did not feel a vain need to spew trauma across the written page; instead, I hope this book has helped to give your voice a voice within mine so that your journey toward recovery may also begin.

God has not forgotten you. He knows your pain and He alone can change your scent of trauma into the scent of heaven.

A promise from God:

*"Can a woman
forget her nursing child, that
she should have no compassion
on the son of her womb?
Even these may forget, yet
I will not forget you."*

Isaiah 49:15 (ESV)

Epilogue

I HOPE THAT, IN RETROSPECT, AS YOU READ MY stories, you can see your experience inside some of mine and that they had meaning to you beyond the words as read from the page. It's amazing how we can connect with each other through our shared experiences, even if we come from different backgrounds or live in different parts of the world. Sometimes, reading someone else's stories can help us make sense of our own lives and find meaning in the things we've gone through.

I needed to remember these things with you so that in remembering them together, we might see the hand of God writ much larger than we may now see Him. It's comforting to know that we're not alone in this world and that there's a greater purpose to everything that happens in our lives. Even when things seem difficult or uncertain, we can find solace in the knowledge that there's a higher power at work, guiding us along the way.

So, as you read my stories, I hope that you found comfort, inspiration, and meaning in them. And who knows? Maybe one day, you'll be able to share your own stories with someone else and help them find their way, too.

The trajectory of my life experience was formed on an August night in 1955, the night when my mom was left for dead. It has taken a lifetime to undo the damage that emanated from that moment. Yet in reading, I trust that you saw hope and growth even from pain.

Trauma created an opening to doubt my own memories and experiences. It was as if I had completely gaslighted myself, and I didn't know what was real anymore. Remembering Melinda from the past allowed me to reach out to her in the present, hoping that she might remember me.

To my relief, Melinda did remember me, and she validated that I was indeed a real boy. My memories were real and accurate. Knowing this gave me a sense of peace and helped me to move past the doubts and fears that had been plaguing me. Looking back, I realize that my nightmares, as bad as they were to experience, were not just phantoms. They were rooted in real experiences that I had gone through. I am grateful to Melinda for helping me to see that and for reminding me of who I really am.

Perhaps you saw that even though my encounter with the nurse couldn't have been more than 30 seconds the memory lingers in clarity until now. It wasn't simply the loss of Bourbon; it was that she was present with me, yet in my pain, I had to remove myself and dissociate from my pain, but the memory of comfort lingers that she was present, even in her tears, or better, especially in her tears.

Growing up in a household that didn't practice any religion led to me becoming an atheist. Yet, even though I did not experience the presence of God in my early life, when things seemed chaotic and out of control, God was, and is, still in charge.

My point is confirmed in Romans 8:28, "And we know that in all things God works for the good of those who love him, who have been called according to his purpose." (NIV) The promise that God works all things together for good does not mean that all things, taken by themselves, are good. Some things and events are decidedly bad. But God has a master plan, sees the big picture, and works them together for our good. That does not mean that we will acquire all that we want or desire. However, since His plan is always for our good, we can take confidence that no matter what our circumstances or contexts are, God is active and will conclude things according to His loving, good, and wise design.

Romans 8:38-39 gives us even more wonderful news, "For I am sure that neither death nor life, nor angels nor rulers, nor things present nor things to come, nor powers, nor height nor depth, nor anything else in all creation, will be able to separate us from the love of God in Christ Jesus our Lord." (ESV) We can trust in God's goodness, power, and will to work out all things for our good as we walk on this journey of recovery with Him.

The Lord bless you
and keep you;
the Lord make his face shine on you
and be gracious to you;
the Lord turn his face toward you
and give you peace.

Numbers 6:24-26 (ESV)

Appendix A

METAMORPHOSES

Ovid
Bk IV: 753–803

Medusa was astonishingly fair;
She was desired and contended for—
so many jealous suitors hoped to win her.
Her form was graced by many splendors,
yet there was no other beauty she possessed
that could surpass the splendor of her hair—
and this I learned from one
who said he'd seen her.
Her beauty led the Ruler of the Sea
To rape her in Minerva's sanctuary
(so goes the tale).
Jove's daughter turned aside chaste eyes:
the goddess hid her face behind her aegis—
but she made Medusa pay:
she changed that Gorgon's hair
to horrid snakes.
And to this day, Minerva, to dismay
and terrify her foes, wears on her breast
the very snakes that she herself had set—
as punishment—upon Medusa's head.

Appendix B

PSALM 100 (KJV)

Make a joyful noise unto the Lord, all ye lands.
Serve the Lord with gladness:
Come before his presence with singing.

Know ye that the Lord he is God:
It is he that hath made us, and not we ourselves.
We are his people, and the sheep of his pasture.

Enter into his gates with thanksgiving,
And into his courts with praise:
Be thankful unto him, and bless his name.

For the Lord is good;
His mercy is everlasting;
And his truth endureth to all generations.

Appendix C

PRIVILEGE WALK ACTIVITY

Albany University (2019). Privilege Walk. http://www.albany.edu/ssw/ efc/pdf/Module%205_1_Privilege %20Walk% 20Activity.pdf.

DIRECTIONS FOR THE ACTIVITY

1. Have participants form a straight line across the room about an arm's length apart, leaving space in front and behind.
2. Read the purpose of this activity to help provide context for the exercise.
3. This workshop has been designed to provide college students with an opportunity to understand the intricacies of privilege and explore how we enjoy benefits based on being members of social identity groups in the United States. Please note that this exercise is not meant to make anyone feel guilty or ashamed of her or his privilege or lack of privilege related to any social identity categories.
4. State the following:
   Listen to the following statements, and follow the instructions given. For example, when I read "If you have blue eyes, take one step forward," only people with blue eyes will move and everyone else will stand still. Each step should be an average length step. This activity should be done in silence.

5. Read the following "Privilege Walk Statements" one at a time, allowing time for participants to take a step forward or back as their answers require.

Privilege Walk Statements

___ If English is your first language, take one step forward.

___ If either of your parents graduated from college, take one step forward.

___ If you have been divorced or impacted by divorce, take one step forward.

___ If there have been times in your life when you skipped a meal because there was no food in the house, take one step backward.

___ If you have visible or invisible disabilities, take one step backward.

___ If you were encouraged to attend college by your parents and family members, take one step forward.

___ If you grew up in an urban setting, take one step backward.

___ If your family had health insurance, take one step forward.

___ If your work and school holidays coincide with religious holidays that you celebrate, take one step forward.

___ If you studied the culture or the history of your ancestors in elementary school, take one step forward.

___ If you have been bullied or made fun of based on something you cannot change (i.e., your gender, ethnicity, age, or sexual orientation), take one step backward.

___ If you were ever offered a job because of your association with a friend or family member, take one step forward.

___ If you have ever felt passed over for an employment position based on gender, ethnicity, age, or sexual orientation), take one step backward.

___ If you were ever stopped or questioned by the police because they felt you were suspicious, take one step backward.

___ If you or your family ever inherited money or property, take one step forward.

___ If you came from a supportive family environment, take one step forward.

___ If one of your parents was ever laid off or unemployed not by choice, take one step backward.

___ If you are a citizen of the United Stated, take one step forward.

___ If you were ever uncomfortable about a joke or statement you overheard related to your race, ethnicity, gender, appearance, or sexual orientation but felt unsafe to confront the situation, take one step backward.

___ If your ancestors were forced to come to the United States not by choice, take one step backward.

___ If you took out loans for your education, take one step backward.

___ If there were more than fifty books in your house growing up, take one step forward.

___ If you have ever felt unsafe walking alone at night, take one step backward.

___ If you are a white male, take one step forward.

Appendix D

How to Become a Child of God

Step 1*:*

Confess that you have sinned and can't get to heaven on your own good works.

> *None is righteous, no, not one; no one understands;*
> *no one seeks for God. All have turned aside;*
> *together they have become worthless;no*
> *one does good, not even one.*
> Romans 3:10–12 (ESV)

> *For all have sinned and fall short of the glory of God.*
> Romans 3:10–12 (ESV)

Step 2:

Realize that the punishment for sin is death.

> *For the wages of sin is death, but the free gift of God*
> *is eternal life in Christ Jesus our Lord.*
> Romans 6:23 (ESV)

Step 3

Accept that Jesus Christ died for your sins and that His death paid the total price for your salvation.

> *But God shows his love for us*
> *in that Christ died for us while we were still sinners.*
>
> Romans 5:8 ESV

Step 4

Anyone who places their trust in Jesus receives the promise of eternal life.

> *Because if you confess with your mouth*
> *that Jesus is Lord and believe*
> *in your heart that God raised him from*
> *the dead, you will be saved.*
> *For with the heart, one believes and is justified,*
> *and with the mouth one confesses and is saved.*
>
> Romans 10:9–10 (ESV)

Step 5

God's gift of salvation through Jesus Christ is everlasting.

> *For I am sure that neither death nor life, nor angels nor rulers,*
> *nor things present nor things to come, nor*
> *powers, nor height nor depth,*
> *nor anything else in all creation, will be able to separate us*
> *from the love of God in Christ Jesus our Lord.*
>
> Romans 8:38–39 (ESV)

Why not pray this to God today? It's simple and free!

Dear Lord Jesus,
I know I am a sinner, and I ask for Your forgiveness.
I believe You died for my sins and rose from the dead.
I turn from my sins and invite You to come into my heart and life.
I want to trust and follow You as my Lord and Savior.
Amen

Welcome to the family!

To all who RECEIVED HIM
to them He gave the right to become

Children of God,
to those who BELIEVE on HIS NAME.
John 1:12 (ESV)

Appendix E

EDDIE AND PTSD

AFTER MUCH RESEARCH, I UNCOVERED THAT during WWII Eddie had served on an auxiliary aircraft carrier and fought with the US Navy in the Pacific Theater. They supported the invasion landings on Roi, Kwajalein, and Eniwetok in the Marshalls. Immediately afterward, they protected the service group refueling fleet ships engaged in the Palau strikes. Arriving they arrived at Espíritu Santo on Vanuatu Island, just south of the Solomon Islands. On April 7, its planes destroyed airfield installations, sank enemy shipping, hammered harbor facilities on Pagan Island, and conducted valuable photographic reconnaissance on Guam.

At that time, he was a part of the flight crew, and I'm not sure how the kamikaze attacks or naval shelling impacted him. Still, I know that soon afterward, he served as a firefighter. One year later, on April 9, Eddie doubtless responded when a crash-landing fighter started a raging fire among the strike-loaded aircraft on the Chenango's deck. According to records, skillful work by the crew saved the ship from severe damage, and they could remain in action off Okinawa until June 11. It then sailed with the rest of the fleet to engage in the final offensive against the Japanese.

Based on all that I have learned about PTSD, Eddie likely suffered terribly. As a police detective, he most likely put himself in chaos and adrenaline-filled situations to replay the dramas of the war, or perhaps even in his own childhood.

.

Appendix F

Below is a sermon that I preached regarding Elijah.

Trauma to Transcendence
I Kings 19:1-21

Good morning. Let us pray.

> Father, Your Word tells us in Proverbs 30 verse five, "Every word of God is flawless; he is a shield to those who take refuge in him." Flawless are your words; so, if there is any fault, it is mine alone. We come here today with hearts and minds prepared to look into your word. We ask that the stresses and complexities of life would dim as we turn our attention to solutions that you so eloquently provide for us. We thank you that in accordance with your word, you hear our prayer, in the name of our Lord Jesus Christ, Amen.

PERHAPS THE MOST DRAMATIC MOMENT OF THE U.S. space program, even more so than the first lunar landing, was the Apollo 13 mission, commanded by James Lovell.[53] His professionalism remains a model for us today in completing the mission even under adverse circumstances. However, this was not his first challenge.

While serving aboard the aircraft carrier USS Shangri-La in the Sea of Japan, Lovell was flying a night mission. The radio signal he had dialed into his transmitter/receiver as a homing beacon was being broadcast from the carrier he was stationed on. As it would happen, someone on the mainland of Japan was transmitting on the same frequency only with a more powerful signal. So, while Lovell thought he was traveling in the right direction, he was actually following a frequency that would take him further away from the ship. Running low on fuel and without sufficient fuel to get to Japan, he faced the deadly prospect of having to ditch his plane into the sea.

Just when it seemed things could not get any worse; Lovell lost all electrical power including the light he had installed to help him read maps at night. After the Apollo 13 mission, a reporter asked him if there had been a time when he had been afraid. This discussion that follows was reenacted in the 1995 Universal Studio's movie Apollo 13:

> "Uh well, I'll tell ya, I remember this one time – I'm in a Banshee at night in combat conditions, so therethere are no running lights on the carrier. It was the Shrangri-La, and we were in the Sea of Japan and my radar had jammed, and my homing signal was gone . . . because somebody in Japan was actually using the same frequency. And so it was - it was leading me from where I was supposed to be. And I'm looking down at a big, black ocean, so I flip on my map light, and then suddenly: zap. Everything shorts out right there in my cockpit. All my instruments are gone. My lights are gone. And I can't even tell now what my altitude is. I know I'm running out of fuel, so I'm thinking about ditching in the ocean. And I, I look down there, and then in the darkness there's this uh, there's this green trail. It's like a long carpet that's just laid out right beneath me. And it was the algae, right? It was that phosphorescent stuff that gets churned up in the wake of a big ship. And it was - it was - it was leading me home. You know? If my cockpit lights hadn't shorted out, there's no way I'd ever been able to see that. So uh, you, uh, never know . . . what . . . what events must transpire to get you home."[54]

If Lovell's lights had not failed, he would not have been able to see the phosphorescent trail that led him back to the carrier. Undoubtedly, he would never have traveled on mission to the moon and become the hero of space exploration that we know today. We would most likely not even know his name.

In essence, the failure of Lovell's lights was actually the answer to his problem. The traumatic incident that Lovell experienced was precisely what led Lovell back to the Aircraft Carrier; then back home. This event, at least in part, was the source of Lovell's calm leadership while on the Apollo 13 mission.

This may sound counter intuitive, but God can and does use our doubt, despair, and depression caused by trauma to take us back home to Himself. It seems that we might face a divine rebuke for such feelings, but far from rebuking us for a lack of faith, He comes to us gently and carefully to restore us.

Have you ever had a time when the circumstances in your life felt so overwhelming that you completely lost sight of hope? Have you ever been so traumatized, or so close to someone who has been, that you have lost sight of God's love? Has there been a time when you could not see the glory of God and could only contemplate the inky blackness of certain doom just as Lovell did?

If you have, then God gives you hope this day. If you have ever felt that way, you are among some of God's wonderful saints who became depressed and isolated. Job 10:18-22 tells us that in the midst of his despair Job cried out, "Why then have You brought me out of the womb? Would that I had died, and no eye had seen me! I should have been as though I had not been, carried from womb to tomb." Years later a prophet of God, Jonah, in Jonah 4:8, begged God with all his soul to let him die after the city of Nineveh repented, saying, "Death is better to me than life." And in our text today we will hear the prophet Elijah call out to God in a moment of deep distress, "O LORD, take my life."

First, I want to tell you that, although it is possible to lead you to sin, being in a state of despair or depression is not a sin. Rather, despair, depression, and losing sight of God and his love after being traumatized or witnessing trauma is, in fact, the normal response. It is how God has created us. Genesis informs us that God created the Garden of Eden as a place for us to dwell in eternal fellowship with each other and with the LORD.

God created us for eternal relationships, communion, and abundant life in harmony with all creation. Therefore, when relationships are broken, when outside forces threaten us, when we fail to be in communion with God, when we are out of harmony with the rest of God's creation, we suffer. Some want to label this suffering as sin, or rather; our response to suffering as sin; but the weight of Scripture tells us that while it is the result of sin in this world, it, in itself, is not.

Let us examine the life of Elijah for a moment, a man so close to God that he did not die but was taken into heaven in a chariot of fire. Yet earlier, Elijah had called out, "... O LORD, take my life ..." If Elijah was such a godly person who faced the depths of despair and depression, then his experience has much to teach us.

To put this time of Elijah's life in proper perspective we need to review what had just happened. James 5:17 tells us that, "[Elijah] earnestly prayed that it might not rain; and it did not rain on the earth for three years and six months." Then, God sent him to appear before King Ahab, and a contest was set up between the living God of Israel and Baal on Mount Carmel. The true God would be the one who consumed the bull sacrifice with fire. The living God of Israel answered with fire, causing many in Israel to declare their faith in the God of Israel alone. Then, Elijah and the godly Jews put the 850 false prophets to death.

Elijah returned to the top of Mount Carmel and prayed again to the living and gracious God Jehovah, "and the sky poured rain, and the earth produced its fruit" (James 5:18). Ahab and Elijah raced back to the palace in Jezreel. Ahab drove his chariot, but Elijah, empowered by the Spirit, outran the king to the city gates. When Ahab arrived at his summer palace in Jezreel he told Jezebel all that had happened. Jezebel immediately planned Elijah's death. A message from her read, "To Elijah, troubler of Israel: So, may the gods do to me and even more, if I do not make your life as the life of one of my dead prophets by tomorrow about this time." Then the Bible tells us of Elijah's response, "And he was afraid ..." Elijah became so afraid he forgot the presence of God.

While most commentators write that Elijah's fear was born of sin, I want to remind you that he had just had the most traumatic experiences of his life. As a military chaplain and former Artillery Forward Observer, I have seen the results of war and it is not pleasant. While conflicts are sometimes necessary, I am reminded of the lone surviving member of the Medal of Honor recipient Michael Murphy's team, Marcus Luttrell, said, "There's a lot of awards in the military, but when you see a Medal of Honor, you know whatever they went through is pretty horrible. You don't congratulate anyone when you see it."[55]

Elijah had been through a traumatic experience and even though God had consumed the bull, and the altar, Ahab and Jezebel still did not repent. Unquestioningly, doubts ran through Elijah's mind. "Have I misunderstood the voice of God that was so clear?" "If I was wrong about this, the most important mission in my life, then what else am I wrong about?" "I am no better than my fathers – they got it wrong and now, so have I." Elijah's conception of his very purpose had changed. In a moment trauma transformed him into a fearful, fleeing prophet. But by this, I mean no judgment at all, only sorrow at the sad state trauma took him to.

Trauma produces the same thing in us as it did in Elijah: a lack of food, water, and sleep, resulting in exhaustion; Jezebel's death threat resulted in disappointment in God, and fear for his life. He left his servant and so then became completely isolated, causing him to cry out to God in total despair. Elijah most likely felt like a complete failure as he fell asleep.

When the man who led me to a personal relationship with Christ, who was a fellow soldier, who stood as my best man at my wedding, who was my business partner, who was my best friend, died suddenly and horribly, Elijah's pain became only too real to me. Perhaps you have felt this pain. Perhaps for you it was the death of someone you loved; maybe it wasn't a physical death. Perhaps it was the death of a relationship or even the death of a dream. Whatever it may be for you, recognize that God made you for community--you were not made for separation, and the pain you feel is the normal response to an abnormal situation.

Yet, there is beauty in Elijah's trauma too. You must recognize this to see God's heart, to see the great love the Lord has for Elijah, and you. After Elijah rested a bit, God sent an angel to tell him to arise and eat. When Elijah awoke, he saw some freshly baked bread and a jar of water.

No, God was not going to take his life as he had requested, or chastise him for his lack of faith, or for being in a sinful state; no, God was going to fed him and put back on his feet gently and gradually.

Max Lucado tells the story of Chippie the parakeet in his book In the Eye of the Storm.

> Chippie the parakeet never saw it coming. One second, he was peacefully perched in his cage. The next he was sucked in, washed up, and blown over. The problems began when Chippie's owner decided to clean Chippie's cage with a vacuum cleaner. She removed the attachment from the end of the hose and stuck it in the cage. The phone rang, and she turned to pick it up. She'd barely said 'hello' when 'sssopp!' Chippie got sucked in. "The bird owner gasped, put down the phone, turned off the vacuum, and opened the bag." There was Chippie-- still alive but stunned. Since the bird was covered with dust and soot, she grabbed him and raced to the bathroom, turned on the faucet, and held Chippie under the running water. Then, realizing that Chippie was soaked and shivering, she did what any compassionate bird owner would do--she reached for the hair dryer and blasted the pet with hot air. "Poor Chippie never knew what hit him." "A few days after the trauma, the reporter who'd initially written about the event contacted Chippie's owner to see how the bird was recovering. 'Well,' she replied, 'Chippie doesn't sing much anymore he just sits and stares.' It's hard not to see why: sucked in, washed up, and blown over . . . that's enough to steal the song from the stoutest heart."[56]

Perhaps your song has been stolen from your heart as well.

Doctors Frank Minrith and Paul Meier, nationally renowned Christian counselors were my pastoral counseling professors at Dallas Seminary. After 25 years, one of their observations still rings clearly in my head; 50% of all emotional difficulties they saw in the hospital setting dissipated simply by allowing the person to get adequate hydration, food, and sleep for about three days. The Lord knows that! The Lord wants you to get adequate water, food, and sleep.

So, yes, Elijah forgot the presence of God in the face of trauma, but God did not forget Elijah. He did not wallop Elijah over the head, and this was not because God owed Elijah some debt of gratitude so that He would treat Elijah differently than He would treat us, God owes no man. No, God told Elijah to go and stand outside the cave. God was about to remind Elijah, through some dramatic phenomena, of His character. "And a great and strong wind was rending the mountains and breaking in pieces the rocks before the LORD, but the LORD was not in the wind" (1 Kings 19:11). God is always present like the wind, and He can use this wind to bring judgment or blessing. But for Elijah God was not in the wind.

Then there was an earthquake, but God was not in the earthquake. God had used an earthquake to judge the rebellion of Korah in the wilderness (see Numbers 16). Earthquakes can shake all the physical foundations of this earth and bring down mountains as well as kingdoms, as they will in the days of the great tribulation. Yet, God was not in the earthquake.

There was fire, but the Lord was not in the fire. In the past, God had used fire to judge the sin of Sodom and to judge the nation of Egypt with fire from heaven the likes of which Egypt had never seen in its recorded history (see Exodus 9:22f). God had appeared before Moses in the burning bush and on Mount Horeb in fire. As well, each night He was a pillar of fire to lead His people through the wilderness. But God was not in the fire.

A traumatized person does not need to hear the thundering of the preacher telling him or her to repent, or just do better, or the shaking of the earth or the burning of the fire – a traumatized person's life has already been shaken and burnt. They do not need to hear of the power of God to be remorseful, nor the power of God to shake, nor the power of God to burn, they need something different. They need what God gave to Elijah, a gentle healing touch.

Finally, there was a sound of a gentle whisper "Elijah, speak with me again." Elijah heard the voice of the Lord, and then he came to the mouth of the cave and the Lord spoke with him a second time with the same question: "Elijah, what are you doing standing here?"

But Elijah was still gripped by his trauma and repeats himself. Such it is with people who have been traumatized, they repeat the event over and over in their minds trying to make sense; why this happened? Why this? Why now? Yet, God comes to Elijah the same way he comes to us with love, truth, and time.

Not only did Elijah's trauma cause him to forget the presence and character of God, but, also God's sovereign rule. In 1 Kings 19:15-21, God gave Elijah some important information, "Elijah, within this idolatrous nation there are seven thousand men and women who will not suffer any judgment from the sword because they have not bowed their knee to Baal nor kissed his statue!" Elijah was not alone; you are not alone.

It is important to know that you are not alone in your trauma. Others have faced similar traumas; each one is on their own journey. You are surrounded by a loving church; by resources that extend all the way to heaven. But, you may not be able to hear the still small voice of God in the midst of the stress you face. Be patient. Be still.

Finally, God told Elijah to, "Go," and he encouraged the prophet by providing him the power to enable him to believe again; to get up out of his trauma induced depression and accomplish three new missions:

1. Anoint Hazael king over Syria
2. Anoint Jehu king over Israel
3. Anoint Elisha as a prophet in his own place

God restored Elijah; God wants to restore you too. Not only that, but God wants to empower you. Restored to spiritual health, Elijah made the choice to obey God's command to "go," and God gave him the power to walk out of the wilderness. God gives us renewed power.

After the apostle Paul and his disciples came out of a very depressing trial in Asia, Paul wrote the Corinthians, found in 2 Corinthians 1: 8-9, the lesson he had learned:

"... we were burdened excessively, beyond our strength, so that we despaired even of life; indeed, we had the sentence of death within ourselves in order that we should not trust in ourselves, but in God who raises the dead; who delivered us from so great a peril of death and will deliver us, He on whom we have set our hope."

James Lovell saw a small gentle glow in the dark ocean far below that brought him home. Today, perhaps you feel far from home. It may be that you have forgotten God's presence, character, and sovereignty. However, like that phosphorescent glow, God is whispering to you now. You know the Lord is there even while your pain tells you otherwise. Listen to the Word of the Lord, it beckons you to come to God, to speak, to share your pain--God is not distant from you. The Son of God knows pain, the pain of rejection, the pain of lost relationships, and the pain of death. Jesus is here and is not silent, He is whispering to you, "Come home child, come home."

Amen.

Appendix G

RESOURCES

How and Where to Get Help

ONE OF THE MOST CRUCIAL THINGS THAT anyone with a mental health concern is to seek help. This becomes even more important after a traumatic experience, like child abuse or interpersonal violence.

National Child Traumatic Stress Network: https://www.nctsn.org/
National Children's Alliance: https://www.nationalchildrensalliance.org/
Kempe Foundation for Prevention of Child Abuse and Neglect:
      https://kempecenter.org/
American Professional Society on the Abuse of Children:
      https://apsac.org/:
International Society for Traumatic Stress Studies:
      https://istss.org/home
Evidence-Based Programs Resource Center:
      https://www.samhsa.gov/resource-search/ebp
National Children's Advocacy Center: https://www.nationalcac.org/
Center on the Developing Child, Harvard University:
      https://developingchild.harvard.edu/science/key-concepts/toxic-stress/
In Texas: TwelveTwo Christian Counseling:
      https://www.twelvetwocounseling.com/

End Notes

1 Robert Graves, *On English Poetry*, 1922 (cited in Schauffler, 1925).

2 Some modern scholars suggest a procession seven kilometers long as plausible. See Beard, 102.

3 Iain Thomas, *I Wrote This for You.*

4 Silver, R. C., Holman, E. A., McIntosh, D. N., Poulin, M., and Gil-Rivas, V. (2002). "A Nationwide Longitudinal Study of Psychological Responses to September 11th." *JAMA: The Journal of the American Medical Association, 288* (10), 1235–1244. doi: 10.1001/jama.288.10.1235. "Recovering Emotionally from Disaster: Understanding the Emotions and Normal Responses That Follow a Disaster or Other Traumatic Event Can Help You Cope with Your Feelings, Thoughts, and Behaviors." https://www.apa.org/_topics/trauma#:~:text=Trauma%20is%20an%20emotional%20response,symptoms%20like%20headaches%20or%20nausea.

5 Staff, *Psychology Today.* "Adverse Childhood Experiences." https://www.psychologytoday.com/us/basics/adverse-childhood-experiences.

6 Ovid's *Metamorphoses.*

7 Miate, Liana Neptune, October 7, 2022, https://www.worldhistory.org/Neptune/#:~:text=Creator%20of%20Horses-,The%20ancient%20Greeks%20attributed%20the%20creation%20of%20horses%20to%20Neptune,right%20to%20name%20the%20city.

8 Bessel Van der Kolk, MD, medical director, the Trauma Center in Boston.

9 Glennon, M. "Medusa in Ancient Greek Art." https://www.metmuseum.org/toah/hd/medu/hd_medu.htm. March 2017.

10 Richman-Abdou, K. "Kintsugi: The Centuries-Old Art of Repairing Broken Pottery with Gold." https://mymodernmet.com/kintsugi-kintsukuroi/. March 5, 2022.

11 https://genius.com/Rain-perry-beautiful-tree-by-rain-perry-lyrics.

12 On November 18, 1992, my mother and stepfather, Norman, were killed in an automobile accident in Sand Point, Idaho.

13 Barton, C. (director). *The Shaggy Dog* (film). Walt Disney Productions, 1959.

14 Stevenson, R. (director). *The Absent-Minded Professor* (film). Walt Disney Productions, 1961.

15 Tewksbury, P. (director). *My Three Sons* (sitcom). CBS Broadcasting, 1960.

16 One of the best depictions of anyone that came close to Eddie was in the movie *I Can Only Imagine.* Dennis Quaid played the father. As one who lived it, if I may, Dennis, your work was profoundly accurate in the areas you allowed your

character to go, especially when you struck the back of his head just out of the blue, for no particular reason. You went dark, probably as dark as a movie audience could handle. As well as you were allowed to portray the darkness; however, there are even darker pathways.

[17] See appendix C for more information about Eddie's military experience. My experience as a chaplain and counselor gives my adult self a measure of understanding for Eddie. I believe that, at least in part, his alcohol use and abuse of Mom and us boys were a result of complex PTSD.

[18] Willis, T. (October 8, 2003). "Weapons Wired for Violence." https://www.baltimoresun.com/news/bs-xpm-2003-10-09-0310090431-story.html.

[19] American Psychiatric Association. (July 2017). *What Is Exposure Therapy?* https://www.apa.org/ptsd-guideline/patients-and-families/exposure-therapy.

[20] Tillich. The Eternal Now. https://www.goodreads.com/quotes/280617-our-language-has-wisely-sensed-these-two-sides-of mans#:~:text=%E2%80%9COur%20language%20has%20wisely%20sensed%20these%20two%20sides%20of%20man's,the%20glory%20of%20being%20alone.%E2%80%9D.

[21] What Does It Mean to Be "Present"? https://manhattanmentalhealthcounseling.com/what-does-it-mean-to-be-present/.

[22] https://m.facebook.com/susandavidphd/photos/your-life-experiences-are-only-as-powerful-are-your-ability-to-turn-them-into-li/464476890611537/.

[23] Albany University. (2019) Privilege Walk. http://www.albany.edu/ssw/efc/pdf/Module%205_1_Privilege%20Walk% 20Activity.pdf.

[24] Attributed to Jenna Evans Welch. https://www.goodreads.com/quotes/9576863-a-good-friend-is-like-a-four-leaf-clover-hard-to.

[25] Fischer, S. (Director). (2013). *Memorial Day* (film). Image Entertainment.

[26] Gray, W. S., Hill, M. A., (1946–47). *Fun with Dick and Jane.* https://www.amazon.com/Dick-Jane-1946-47-William-Gray/dp/B00908EAZO.

[27] See appendix C.

[28] See appendix D.

[29] Seteanu, S. L., and Giosan, C. (2021). "Adverse Childhood Experiences in Fathers and the Consequences in Their Children." *Professional Psychology: Research and Practice, 52*(1), 80–89. https://doi.org/10.1037/pro0000360.

[30] George Eliot. "Don't judge a book by its cover."

[31] https://www.bethelelc.com/belc-blog/childhood-amnesia.

[32] Carrie Bradshaw. https://20quotes.com/38372_i-wasn-t-searching-for-something-or-someone.

[33] Van der Kolk. https://20quotes.com/38372_i-wasn-t-searching-for-something-or-someone.

[34] True Colors. https://20quotes.com/38372_i-wasn-t-searching-for-something-or-someone.

[35] Hayim Ben-Sasson, ed., A History of the Jewish People (Cambridge, Massachusetts: Harvard University Press, 1985), 122.

36 Duane Howell and Susan H. Howell, "Journey to Mount Horeb1-18: Cognitive Theory and First Kings 19," Journal of Mental Health, Religion and Culture 2, no. 7 (November 2008): 655.

37 Abraham H. Maslow, "A Theory of Human Motivation," Psychological Review 50 (1943): 370-96.

38 The American Heritage Medical Dictionary, (Boston, Massachusetts: Houghton Mifflin Harcourt, 2007), s.v. "Rest."

39 "VA/DOD Clinical Practice Guidelines RSS News Feed," U.S. Department of Veterans Affairs, http://www.healthquality.va.gov (accessed January 11, 2011).

40 John F. Tillery, "Pastoral Counseling." (Pastoral Counseling, Pt. 2, class lecture notes) (Dallas, Texas: Dallas Theological Seminary, 1982).

41 Note: Additional appearances of the Angel of the Lord are also seen in Genesis 16:7-14; Genesis 22:11-15; Genesis 31:11-13; Exodus 3:2-4; Numbers 22:22-38; Judges 2:1-3; Judges 6:11-23; and Judges 13:3-22.

42 Hugh Pope, ed., The Catholic Encyclopedia (New York, New York: Robert Appleton Company, 1907), s.v. "Angels."

43 Department of Defense, US Army Survival Manual: FM 21-76 (Washington D.C.: Department of the Army, 1970), 63.

44 Note: See also Exodus 19:16, 18; Jude 4:4-5; 2 Samuel 22:8-16; Psalm 18:7-15; 68:8; Hebrews 12:18.

45 Judith Lewis Herman, M.D., Trauma and Recovery: The Aftermath of Violence--from Domestic Abuse to Political Terror, 14th printing ed. (New York, New York: Basic Books, 1997), 1-10.

46 Norman R. Davies, "Elijah and the Peace of Jerusalem," Jewish Contemplatives, http://jewishcontemplatives.blogspot.com/2010/04/elijah-and-peace-of-jerusalem-lag-bomer.html (accessed February 16, 2011).
    Note: Norman Davies is a dedicated Jewish contemplative, i.e., a Jewish monk.

47 Ibid.

48 Dr. C. George Boreree, "Sigmund Freud," Personality Theories, http://webspace.ship.edu/cgboer/freud.html (accessed February 15, 2011).
    Note: Freud seemed fond of the phrase and used it in his lecture.

49 Bessel A. Van der Kolk, M.D., "The Compulsion to Repeat the Trauma: Reenactment Victimization and Masochism," Psychiatric Clinics of North America 12 (1989): 389-411.
    Note: Reenactment is a term used to describe the lingering behavioral enactment and automatic repetition of the past. The very nature of traumatic information processing determines the reenactment behavior. The traumatized person is cut off from language, deprived of the power of words, trapped in speechless terror.

50 Bessel A. Van der Kolk, M.D., "The Psychological Processing of Traumatic Experience: Rorschach Patterns in PTSD," Journal of Traumatic Stress 2 (1989): 259-74.

51 Van der Kolk.

52   Alcoholics Anonymous. https://20quotes.com/38372_i-wasn-t-searching-for-something-or-someone.

53   "Jim Lovell," Wikipedia, http://en.wikipedia.org/wiki/Jim_Lovell (accessed January 12, 2011).

54   "Apollo 13 (film)," Wikiquote, http://en.wikiquote.org/wiki/Apollo_13 (accessed January 12, 2011).

55   Associated Press, "Bush Awards Medal of Honor to Navy Seal," White House on MSNBC, http://www.msnbc.msn.com/id/21418436/ns/politics-white_house/ (accessed January 23, 2011).

56   Max Lucado, In the Eye of the Storm (Nashville, Tennessee: Thomas Nelson, 2002), 11.

References

Beard, M. (2007). The Roman Triumph. London, Belknap Press.

English Standard Version Bible. (2001). ESV Online. https://esv.literalword.com/.

King James Bible. (2008). Oxford University Press. (Original work published 1769.)

Mandelbaum, A. (October 1, 1993) The Metamorphoses of Ovid: A New Verse Translation. Boston: Mariner Books.

Seteanu, S. L., and Giosan, C. (2021). "Adverse Childhood Experiences in Fathers and the Consequences in Their Children." Professional Psychology: Research and Practice, 52(1), 80–89. https://doi.org/10.1037/pro0000360.

The Holy Bible, New International Version. (1984). Grand Rapids: Zondervan Publishing House.

Thomas, I. S. (2018). I Wrote This for You. Kansas City, Missouri: Andrews McMeel Publishing.

Van der Kolk, B. A. (2015). The Body Keeps the Score: Brain, Mind, and Body in the Healing of Trauma. New York: Penguin Books.

About the Author

Dr. J. Franklin Tillery is currently the pastor of a church in Texas. He and his wife, Barbara, have lived in five countries and moved over thirty-two times, but after forty-seven years of marriage, they have finally put down roots!

Before retiring from the military in 2016, he served on a forward observer team in the US Army Field Artillery (1972–1976). He began his ministry among the Plymouth Brethren in 1977. During his pastoral career, he served as the associate pastor of the Arab Church of Dallas (1984–1987); pastor of Denali Bible Chapel in Fairbanks, Alaska (1987–1991); academic dean of the Jordanian Evangelical Theological Seminary (1991–1992) and pastor of the International Church in Amman, Jordan (1992–1996).

In 1996, he joined the United States Air Force as a chaplain. During his Air Force career, he served at nine duty stations and deployed in support of Operations Northern Watch, Southern Watch, Desert Fox, Joint Forge, and Unified Protector. He also provided direct combat support during Operation Inherent Resolve.

Through the power of God, though he never stepped foot in a high school as a student, in 1981, he received his GED and a bachelor's degree in secondary education. He has since earned four master's degrees and a doctorate.

Milton Keynes UK
Ingram Content Group UK Ltd.
UKHW040928020924
447770UK00002B/200

9 798823 017640